Family Divorce Therapy 101

A Clinician's Guide to Best Practices for Treating Families Pre/During/Post Divorce

BY

TRANSITIONS RESOURCE, LLC

Preface

As divorce rates continually climb (US statistics quote ranges in 45-50% of marriages 14 years or older result in divorce) this ever growing population will be seeking your services. As a Clinician, a good solid understanding of what they may experience through the divorce process will enhance your ability to help them. Your clients will come to you in various stages of pre-divorce consideration, during the process and post divorce. The guidance herein can be adapted to all of these stages.

A large portion of this book is focused on the wounding that results in costly drawn out litigated divorce cases. When a marriage is irreparable there is a great need to buffer those family members from an additional layer of pain and suffering that can be caused through the litigious legal divorce process. A family already devastated by a failed relationship between spouses should be aware that they can benefit from resources available to them to avoid very costly common pitfalls. Most of the conflict and wounding can be greatly reduced by seeking out low conflict alternative methods of divorce. Family Mediation Centers can offer these alternative methods and we strongly encourage you to refer your clients to these centers prior to them hiring an Attorney and engaging in the traditional legal process that can be so devastating. These centers provide teams of professionals including financial planners, mediators and attorneys that are dedicated to serving families the most efficient way possible.

Many family members incur long term devastating debt and develop post traumatic stress disorder brought on by a high conflict, litigated divorce. Often these families can never emotionally recover. Our mission is to provide you, the Clinician with tools and resources for you to empower these families to make wise decisions that will springboard the family into a healthy post divorce mindset. This book is a compilation of contributions from a variety of professionals, all experts in family therapy with an extended tenure serving in their respective fields.

The primary content in this book was created by a team of licensed professionals for the Family Divorce Continuing Education Series that has been accredited by the Licensed Professional Counselors Association (LPCA) and the National Association of Social Workers (NASW) and featured at their annual state conferences and conventions in Georgia since 2010. With permission we have also incorporated content from the *Children of Divorce* Co-Parenting Seminar required by most Georgia Counties, published and trademarked by Jeri Apple (Amann) and Marti Kitchens.

A special thank you to contributors/past presenters Kelley Linn, Publisher, Founder Transitions Resource, LLC; Leslie Dinkins-Perez, LCSW; Dawn Echols, MS, LPC, GA Registered Mediator; Marti Kitchens, MA, LMFT, LPC, GA Registered Mediator; Jeri Apple (Amann), LCSW, LMFT; Kathleen Shack, LMFT; Denise Houston, LPC; Andria Palmer, LMSW; Dr. Lisa Cheyette, PhD; Amy Bear, LPC, Author; Dr. Jessica Blalock, PhD and the past and current staffs of the Georgia Licensed Professional Counselors Association (GA LPCA) and National Association of Social Workers- GA Chapter (NASW). Their professional support of this very important work to serve families of divorce to help minimize financial and emotional wounding and enhance healing is greatly appreciated.

We have included references within this book to other multiple publications by Transitions Resource, LLC. These references are not intended to be self-serving. These publications were created by our team of professionals as additional tools for Clinicians to have in their toolbox above and beyond other nationally recognized resources you may already be using. We welcome your suggestions on additional resources.

www.TransitionsDivorcePrep.com / www.DivorceMediationCenter.org

Family Divorce Therapy 101

A Clinician's Guide to Best Practices when Treating Families Pre/During/Post Divorce

CONTENTS

AVERAGE TIMELINE/COSTS

Litigated Divorce Process:

Prep for Case	Securing Counsel	Negotiation	Mediation	Hearing
Establish records, logs and evidence (Transitions Workbook)	Interview candidates Select Counsel	Negotiate btwn Opposing Counsel 1-4 weeks	1, 2, 3 sessions 4-8 weeks	Hearing Date Established Evidence Prepared Depositions Taken Hearing conducted
		Prep of Settlement Documents/filing 2-5 weeks	Prep of Settlement Documents/filing 2-5 weeks	
		If no resolution reached then Mediations req'd	If no resolution reached then Hearing req'd	
6-24 months	2-3 weeks	3-9 weeks	6-13 weeks	2-6 months **
Average fees	($2500-$5000) retainer due for initial filing only	+	($2500-$8000) +	($5000-$50,000)

** Final Judgment and Divorce Decree Issued　　　　　　　　**Average total $45,000 - $50,000**

3 weeks-12 months depending on jurisdiction (county case is filed in) and caseload of Judge

This is the traditional process of a divorce. If you have hired an Attorney who overlooks the negotiation and mediation stage of your process within the first 30 days of retaining them and insists on heading straight for litigation, request a refund of your retainer and *seek alternative representation as soon as possible*. Litigated divorces will cost a family an average of $50,000 but have ranged into the hundreds of thousands of dollars and will usually create long-term debt and emotional conflict between spouses that may be irreparable.

AVERAGE TIMELINE/COSTS

Transitions Mediated Divorce Process:

Prep for Case	See CPA	Mediate	Attorney Preps Docs	File Documents
Meet with Coach Collect info	Have financial options recommended	with 2 Attorneys present 1-3 Sessions		
		Prep of Settlement Documents 1-3 weeks		
1-2 months	1-3 weeks	3-6 weeks if multiple mediations	1-2 weeks	2-6 months **
Final Judgment and Divorce Decree Issued		Average total $3,500-$7,500		
Average fees	($1700-$2000) +	($1500-$4500) +	($500-$1,000)	($200)

A **significantly less costly alternative process rapidly spreading across the U.S. is being offered by Family Divorce Mediation Centers for usually less than $7,000. They offer facilitators, financial advisors and mediator/attorney teams during mediation that can finalize the divorce filing documents for a dramatically lower cost, saving families $40,000 - $45,000. We urge families to seek out these centers and explore this alternative method **PRIOR** to securing separate attorneys. This method is less costly than both the "collaborative" or "litigated" divorce processes and minimizes conflict and expense which sets the stage for healthy post divorce relations.

Minimizing Adult Wounding of Divorce (Realigning Expectations)

Edited by Leslie Dinkins-Perez, LCSW

As shown in the divorce process diagram, when a family chooses the traditional approach to divorce by hiring attorneys, filing a petition for divorce and litigating a settlement the risk for great emotional distress and financial devastation increases.

What are some truths most Attorneys won't reveal when hired for divorce services?

o   The retainer they require is simply a deposit toward fees and that the average cost of a litigated divorce in the United States ranges from $45,000 to $50,000 but can cost up to six figures.

o   Once the family officially submits divorce filing documents to the county courthouse a Judge is assigned the case and the clock starts ticking on billable hour opportunities for the Attorneys. Many counties require regular court appearances every 30-60 days called "Status Conferences" which are very costly for the family and big paydays for Attorneys ($1500-$3000 per status conference).

- A large percentage (98%) of divorce cases settle through mediation just days before a trail is set to occur, usually after many status conferences and several days of depositions are taken from both parties (another costly process for the family and big paydays for Attorneys ($3000-$15,000).

- A family can actually avoid all of the above mentioned costs and submit the filing petition for divorce documents *and* mediated settlement documents simultaneously to completely avoid the costly status conferences and depositions related to a litigated divorce process.

- A party will not get a "better" settlement if they litigate. The litigious judicial process is only designed to help a family separate assets and arrange a custodial plan for the children, it cannot impose financial "punishment" or "rewards" to a party based on ethical or moral relational issues that caused the breakdown of the marriage. The only parties who "win" in a litigated divorce are the Attorneys.

Most of the common emotional wounding resulting from divorce is due to what many people *assume* and *naively expect* from the court process in a variety of areas. When these common assumptions set unrealistic expectations they can have mild to severe emotional repercussions. Avoiding the legal litigious arena altogether by mediating a settlement through a Family Divorce and Mediation Center (who offer the proper professional assistance) greatly enhances the couple's ability to move past divorce and into a more stable financial and emotional co-parenting relationship if they have children together.

Common Unrealistic Expectations from the Court System:

Assumption 1: *When the divorce request is filed someone has to leave the marital home immediately.* This is not so, the couple either needs to agree on separate living arrangements or involve the costly and lengthy legal process to have a Judge order one of the partners to leave the marital home.

Assumption 2: *When divorce is filed someone is immediately responsible for child support.* Again either the couple agrees on temporary financial issues to maintain the family obligations or they involve the costly and lengthy legal process to have a Judge order support.

Assumption 3: *If I state a fact in court, my word is proof enough.* In a court of law, facts must be proven with tangible evidence to support them. Judges rely on hard evidence to make all decisions and are more likely to disregard any statements or claims that aren't supported with evidence.

Assumption 4: *The divorce should be officially finalized within about 3 months of filing.* Depending on the method used and the professionals hired, cases can continue well past 3 months and can even extend over many years if litigious professionals encourage conflict (to benefit by increasing billable hours). If a family chooses to mediate their settlement a realistic time frame can range from 2-6 months if multiple mediations are required due to complicated family assets.

Assumption 5: *There are things that the court system just 'knows' as common sense.*
Attorneys carry a caseload average of 10-30 clients at any given time and rarely retain all of the information pertaining to a specific case. When litigating a divorce it is in the client's best interest to keep key bullet points cleanly typed into a brief synopsis of their case and have their attorney review them just prior to entering the courtroom. Judges see hundreds of cases per month and rarely retain any facts specific to a family's situation. Additionally, the Court relies on what can be proven and presented as evidence.

Assumption 6: *They will have unlimited time in court to argue their case.* Due to the number of cases assigned to a Judge per day, each case has a very limited time with the Judge and witnesses will usually only have a few minutes on the stand to answer the most pertinent questions of the issue at hand.

Assumption 7: *They can have an unlimited amount of witnesses.* Actually, only one or two witnesses are usually allowed to provide evidence to prove a point and the witness testimony must be brief and to the point. Most attorneys know this and request witness affidavits be submitted as an alternative to witness testimonials in court.

Assumption 8: *Any piece of paper they bring with them to court will be able to be admitted as evidence.* There are specific guidelines as to what type of document can be submitted as evidence into the court records.

Assumption 9: *Once something is decided on in court, mediation, or a settlement, that it cannot change.* Additional legal action can result in altered court orders.

Assumption 10: *The only financial fees they are responsible for are their Attorney fees.* When a party requests services of a Guardian-Ad-Litem for minor children or for the court to order a full forensic psychological assessment of their spouse, the costs for these services which can vary greatly could range from $5000 to well over $100,000 and the family is obligated to pay for these services once they are court ordered. Usually the parties are mutually financially responsible for any costs that are not independent. This means that most of the time, parties have to pay 50/50 for a Mediator, Guardian-Ad-Litem, Forensic Psychologist and Co-parenting counselor, etc…We have interviewed families who have been burdened with hundreds of thousands of dollars in professional fees for these services.

Assumption 11: *The court will "make" their spouse accountable for their "wrongdoing" and "justice" will be served with punishment.* This is the biggest misconception of all when it comes to a person who feels they have been "wronged" and they want to punish their spouse. The Judge's only goal and assignment is to uphold the law in regards to dividing family assets and arranging a shared parenting plan. They do not make decisions based on unethical or immoral behavior of one of the parties. It is not uncommon for a partner to *believe* that their spouse will be ordered to "pay royally for their mistake" when they go to court; however this is simply not true. In the end the only ones "punished" are the two partners at the cost of their hard earned family funds on unnecessary professional fees.

Common Unrealistic Expectations from their Lawyer

Assumption 1: *Their lawyer is their therapist.* While many attorneys are sympathetic to their client's cause, they are not trained professional counselors that have the skills to emotionally assist the client with psychological issues. A client can rack up enormous legal bills venting to their attorney when in fact they should be bringing these issues to their counselor to sort out. Make your client aware of the financial pitfalls of engaging their attorney in emotional conversations that have no bearing on the legalities of their case. Remind them to call or email you in these cases rather than their attorney who charges $300-$500 per hour of time.

Assumption 2: *Their lawyer will remember every detail of their case.* As stated before the attorney caseload is such that a client needs to be pro-active in reminding their representative of the facts in their case when addressing issues in mediation or court.

Assumption 3: *Their lawyer will bring up every detail of their case in court and mediation.* As stated before, time is limited in court and only pertinent details and evidence will be presented relevant to the issue at hand.

Assumption 4: *That the initial Attorney retainer fee is all they needed to spend and they will be divorced when that fee is consumed.* Retainer fees are simply a starting point to a litigated divorce, once Attorneys are engaged and the divorce is filed there is a process of required court appearances and conferences with the Judge that can dramatically increase the costs. The average litigated divorce costs range from $35,000 to $65,000 or more for a family with simple assets.

Assumption 5: *When they tell their lawyer they don't have any more money that their lawyer won't charge them from that point on but still work on their case.* Simply stated an attorney only provides services that are paid for. Regardless of how sympathetic they are to a client, their time is their means to an income and when a client can no longer pay for their time they will no longer spend billable hours on their case or in some cases will continue to bill hours and after the case is completed will demand payment. If the lawyer is not paid, they have the right to hold a client's evidence, take out liens on a client's assets or receive judgments against their client.

Common Unrealistic Expectations from their Spouse, In-Laws and Extended Family

Assumption 1: *They will tell the truth in every proceeding.* Many spouses are shocked, even devastated when their soon-to-be-Ex makes outlandish, ridiculous, slanderous remarks and claims regarding their character, habits, behavior. Or when their spouse provides financial information that is grossly lacking legitimate numbers. A common rule of thumb is if there has been deception in the marriage, you can bet there will be deception during the divorce.

Assumption 2: *They will be arrested for perjury if they don't tell the truth.* This very rarely happens, the only "truth" the Judge will consider is what is supported with documented evidence.

Assumption 3: *If their in-laws have been on their side in marital issues, in court, the in-laws will still be on their side and tell the truth.* What a spouse's close and extended relatives say in court or claim in affidavit documents usually lean in favor of those they are related to, despite their previous relationship with both partners' pre-divorce filings. The old adage "blood is thicker than water" holds true as these relatives know once the divorce is final they will still maintain a relationship with their own blood and may not consider the consequences they impose on the soon to be ex-spouse.

Assumption 4: *If they blame themselves for their spouse's issues, then when the divorce is filed they will expect their spouse to suddenly become reasonable about all matters because the source of the problem (your self blaming client) is gone.* Most assume once they file for divorce all the angst of the relationship will disappear because they are finally "giving their spouse what they wanted" by divorce. They feel that it will be the end of all of the trouble, and they will immediately start to experience relief, but actually *even more* trouble begins with the litigious legal process and can escalate to unbelievably challenging levels and usually won't settle down until well after settlements have been finalized. Divorcing families need to understand that things will get worse before they get better and they need to prepare themselves for this uphill battle well before they start it.

Assumption 5: *If they are dependent on the spouse for food, shelter, day to day living expenses, insurance, etc. that the spouse would never cut those off.* Sadly some spouses can be horribly vindictive and strategize that by severing access to basic means of survival they can then have some sort of advantage and force their partner into an unfair settlement agreement.

Assumption 6: *The spouse will follow everything in the court paperwork and orders.* Families need to recognize that a person will be more motivated to carry out and fulfill in good faith those items that they personally had a say in and agreed to do, not those that a third party (Judge) ordered them to do. Simply getting a court order for child support or alimony does not necessary mean these will be received. Dead-beat spouses know full well how difficult and costly it is to return to court to enforce a court ordered decree. The family will fare much better when the parties mediate a settlement that serves both of their needs, where both parties have input and make commitments they can live with.

Assumption 7: *Everyone (spouse, in laws, extended family members) will put all their adult issues aside and focus on what is in the best interests of the kids.* Far too often the legal divorce arena brings out the most immature, vindictive nature of a tense-filled relationship and the children are caught in the crossfire. This is one reason why a professionally trained counselor who is a registered mediator can be so productive in mediation. They have the learned skilled sets to identify the unhealthy communication and can diffuse it should negotiation discussions start to head south.

The harsh reality is the judicial system in civil divorce cases is only designed to uphold the laws of the state regarding the dissolution of family assets and designing a contract for issues regarding children. It rarely passes judgment on the moral or ethical behaviors that lead to the breakdown of the family relationship. The legal outcome of a trial is extremely unpredictable. We have heard many stories from clients post divorce who spent $50,000 – $100,000 preparing for trial only to be told by a Judge to "Go back out into the hallway, resolve your differences and do not report back to the court until a resolution between parties is reached". So why engage in a lengthy, costly, additionally wounding process if the outcome will be the same if families sit down and settle their differences up front?

Your client may make one or more or all of these assumptions that can easily lead to being emotionally derailed through the process. When any or all of these assumptions are faced with harsh reality and expectations are unfulfilled, the individual will naturally grieve the loss of these realities. Regardless of whether their relationship with their spouse is high or low conflict there is a natural grieving that comes with divorce, much like that of the loss of anything great such as a job, a loved one, etc. The common areas of divorce grief include:

- The loss of their idea of their future (loss of the "happily ever after" dream)
- Loss of a companion and/or friend
- Loss of hope that the relationship can recover
- Their idea of what they wanted for their children
- Concern over how they will handle daily life moving forward
- Loss of time they spent in the marriage in general
- Loss of time they will spend with their children in shared custody
- Loss of money and material things
- Loss of marital residence
- Loss of friends and social engagements
- Loss of in-laws
- Loss of familiarity with someone and predictable daily routines
- The loss of the idea of who they thought their partner was (versus the reality of who their partner actually is)

In a low conflict divorce someone may be grieving all of the aforementioned ideals; however, there are usually patterns that are able to remain intact:

- Co-parenting of the children and both spouses acting towards the best interests of the children
- Talking civilly to their ex partner about divorce matters
- Staying friends with their ex and/or still wanting each other to be happy and succeed in life
- Having a cordial/friendly relationship with their in-laws
- Maintaining the same friend group

In a high conflict divorce, one or both parties are out to punish or destroy the other. This can lead to issues such as:

- Emotional isolation
- Financial instability or even poverty
- Destruction of reputation and friendships
- Concerns for safety of self or children
- Mild Trauma to Severe PTSD
- Depression, Anxiety
- Internalization of prolonged high stress leading to health concerns and problems

Additionally when preparing someone who has little to no experience with the court system for the process of a high conflict divorce, we work with them to grieve these areas:

- their idea of the judicial system (their expectations versus reality)
- their idea of relief (their expected outcome versus realistic outcome)
- their idea of how they pictured their immediate future to be for both themselves and their children

The factors affecting their emotional response to high conflict and/or trauma include:

- *Expectations* have an enormous effect on how someone processes and reacts to an event, as well as, how they move through grief

- *Internal locus of control:* They believe that control of what happens lies within them, not with sources outside of them

- *Self efficacy:* A sense of confidence in their own coping ability

- *Coherence:* The recognition that even seriously traumatic events are understandable, manageable and meaningful

- *Hardiness & Strength*

- *Frame of Reference:* Their knowledge of divorce based on others experiences

But what if they have no frame of reference? Or if their expectation frame of reference is based on someone's experience close to them with a completely different set of relational dynamics?

Acceptance of the realistic situation is a key factor

Acceptance is the final stage of grief and loss and is necessary to move through difficult feelings and situations into purposeful forward action. The other stages of grief are denial, anger, bargaining and sadness. In many situations people stay in the bargaining stage because the sadness seems overwhelming. Bargaining is trying to manipulate the situation to be what you want it to be or trying to make sense of it when there may be no sense to be made.

A good analogy of moving to acceptance is this scenario:

If you woke up in the night and your kitchen was ABLAZE on fire, past the point of a bucket of water or fire extinguisher, what would you do?

Certainly you would be grieving; grieving the idea of a good night's sleep, grieving the idea of safety in your home, grieving the loss of your kitchen and possibly your house.

But if you were stuck in the bargaining stage you would stand on the edge of the fire saying things like, "Why is the kitchen on fire?", "The kitchen should NOT be on fire!", "This isn't fair!", "If I were the kitchen I wouldn't be on fire!", "I am not moving from this spot until we figure out WHY the kitchen is on fire!". All of that sounds pretty ridiculous, doesn't it? To stand stagnant on the edge of a fire asking questions that don't change the fact that the kitchen is indeed ON FIRE. If you didn't move from that spot you would burn up! Yet that's what we do in bargaining, we ask why and say how it should be rather than accepting that things are the way they are and all the "why's" and "should's" in the world won't change that.

Acceptance doesn't mean we are happy about the situation or that we are comfortable with it or that we don't try to change our involvement. It just means we accept that it is what it is. The kitchen is on fire, accept it, get out of the house, and call the fire department.

You cannot properly deal with a situation until you call it for what it is. If you are unsure of what it is, look at the history, track record, and probability or learn more about what you're up against if the situation is new. You make the call on what's acceptable and how you will determine your boundaries, whether they are emotional, physical, and financial, etc... But remember, "why's" and "should's" will keep you stuck from moving forward. Just get out of the kitchen!!

- Guide your clients to figure out what they want for themselves and their children in the divorce process; what is their objective? What is their bottom line? Help them to stick to that objective and bottom line throughout the process. When they get sidetracked with reactions to behaviors by their spouse or tedious details of the divorce process first validate their feelings but then redirect them back to their basic objectives.

- Guide them to resources that can help them learn whether their objective is realistic and obtainable or simply idealistic

- Help them grieve their expectations of the legal process that aren't realistic and get to a place of acceptance

- Help keep their expectations focused on realities and not potentials; i.e. if their spouse has never been generous with money during the marriage , they will most likely *still* not be generous during a divorce

"If it's that bad, why doesn't she *just* leave?"

Praxis – Rural Technical Assistance on Violence Against Women

The following graphics explain the complicated processes of:

A domestic violence arrest of an abuser

Child protection via Department of Family and Child Services

Securing temporary housing for the victim and children

Obtaining a temporary protective order for the victim

Securing child custody for the non-abusive parent

DOMESTIC VIOLENCE/ARREST INCIDENT

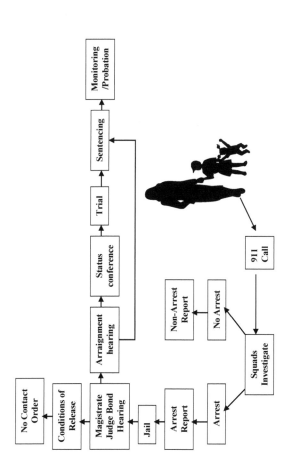

Praxis – Rural Technical Assistance on Violence Against Women

CHILD PROTECTION MAP

Flowchart contents:

- Ongoing case management
- CD Assessment / Psych/Mental Health / Parenting Education / Visitation / Individual/Family Therapy / DV Classes
- Child placed in foster care
- 72 hour emergency hearing
- Court Ordered Case Plan
- 10 day Adjudicatory/Disposition
- Judicial Review
- Substantiated Open file
- Substantiated Closed file
- Assessment / Safety Assessment / Safety plan / Risk Assessment.
- CP Investigation (24 hour or 5 day)
- Law Enforcement Notified
- Child Protection Screening
- Initial Intervention Unit Contacted

Praxis – Rural Technical Assistance on Violence Against Women

HOUSING MAP

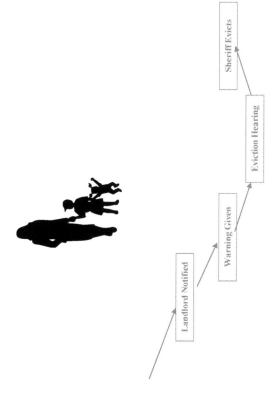

Landlord Notified

Warning Given

Eviction Hearing

Sheriff Evicts

Praxis – Rural Technical Assistance on Violence Against Women

ORDER FOR PROTECTION – CIVIL COURT PROCESS

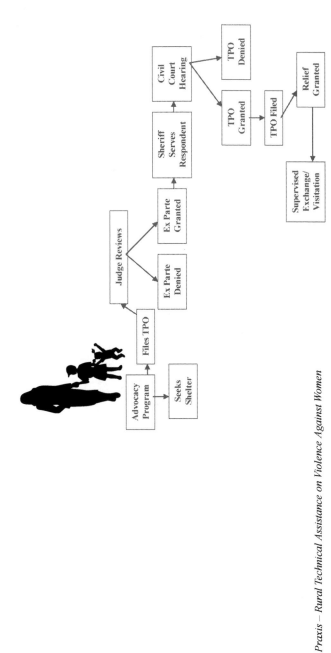

Praxis – Rural Technical Assistance on Violence Against Women

CUSTODY MAP

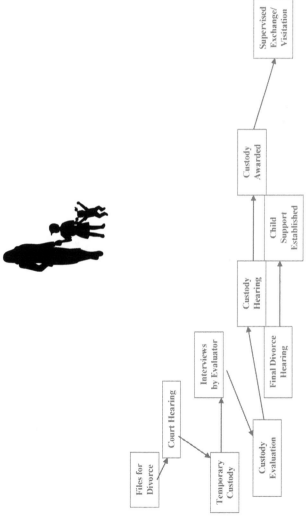

Files for Divorce → Court Hearing → Temporary Custody → Custody Evaluation → Interviews by Evaluator → Custody Hearing → Final Divorce Hearing → Child Support Established → Custody Awarded → Supervised Exchange/Visitation

Praxis – Rural Technical Assistance on Violence Against Women

The below image combines all the processes to "just leave the abuser" to seek safety

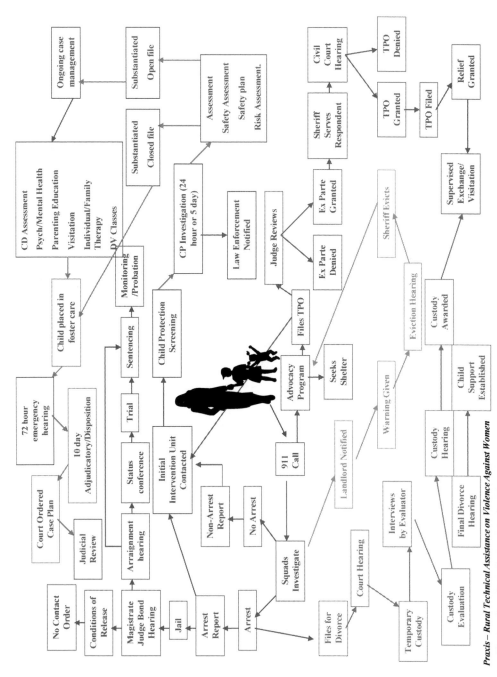

Praxis – Rural Technical Assistance on Violence Against Women

Empowering Clients with Education & Resources

Edited by Kelley Linn, Advocate

National averages of a litigated divorce take 12 to 17 months to complete and cost families $45,000 to $50,000. Why so long and why so much? Because most families do not understand the legal divorce process, do not properly prepare before engaging an Attorney and are uneducated on alternative less costly forms of resolution and settlement. *"You don't know what you don't know, but what you don't know can cost you thousands."*

Additional causes of costly and lengthy cases include:

- A spouse withholds family financial info which takes months/years and substantial professional fees to recover (legally and forensically)

- A spouse insists on a custody battle over minor children -usually financially rooted in a desire to minimize (pay) or maximize (receive) child support payment obligations

- Some litigious Attorneys keep their clients in the dark about the process to enhance the conflict level and intentionally stretch the process out to increase need for their services and billable hours

Atlanta Family Law Attorney Kim Schouller quotes: "What people usually don't know but need to know before they hire an Attorney is there are basically two types of Attorneys, there are "Litigators" and "Negotiators". With Litigators the outcome is a winner and a loser and the focus is on winning at the cost of the other side. With Negotiators the outcome is a winner and a winner and the focus is on finding a solution that meets the needs of all sides. Litigator Attorneys will cost a family $30,000 to over $100,000 for their services, while Negotiator Attorneys will cost a family $3,000 to $15,000 to finalize a divorce."

It's important to remind our clients that the judicial system in civil cases is only designed to uphold the laws in the state to reach a fair financial distribution of family assets and design a parenting contract for children. It makes no mention of moral or ethical behaviors between spouses. When a divorce case makes it into court a judge rarely punishes a spouse for immoral or inappropriate behavior nor passes judgment on the issues that lead to the breakdown of the relationship.

A family has two options. They can mediate a fair settlement of assets and participate in deciding how their child custody will be shared or they can waste thousands of dollars litigating only to end up with exactly the same settlement short of what they wasted in professional fees. Court ordered settlements are rarely upheld by defiant spouses. A couple who has the benefit to decide on their own what they are willing and able to provide (not ordered to) and how to share the children is the couple who usually has the healthiest post divorce co-parenting relations.

The 3 key steps to reduce the additional wounding and high conflict of divorce are:

1) Proper preparation with appropriate professionals (financial/mediation/legal professionals)

2) Seek out a Family Mediation Center and mediate a settlement with a Mediator and negotiation friendly style Attorneys

3) Address emotional issues with a Therapist and only legal issues with the Attorney

What is Proper preparation?

Transitions Resource has published a comprehensive preparation guide entitled *"Transitions Divorce Prep Workbook"* that gives a family a detailed step-by-step process of how to prepare before they engage in the litigious legal process. The workbook is a compilation of professional advice from financial and legal specialists as well as instructions based on hundreds of interviews from families post-divorce and includes how to avoid costly pitfalls.

Proper preparation includes:

1. Understanding the alternative methods of divorce, phases and costs of each method

2. Gathering all relevant financial information and documents and researching multiple settlement options with a financial expert

3. Preparing both spouses for financial independence and stability before the family separates

4. Assessing practical considerations regarding the family home (often the family's largest asset)

5. Preparing custodial logs as a benchmark for an effective parenting plan that minimizes the disruption and impact on the children

6. Reviewing a sample parenting plan and putting thought into how to meet the needs of quality parenting time with both parents and children's specific rituals and already established activities

7. What to do if domestic violence is an issue in the family

8. Steps to take to ensure the family hires negotiation style attorneys representing both parties and strategies on how to maximize time with the Attorneys while minimizing professional fees

9. Understanding the financial and emotional impact of the differences between a mediated or litigated settlement method

10. Completing comprehensive monthly budget expense worksheets for both spouses (including researching changes in expenses such as insurances: medical, auto, home owner/rental insurance and anticipated expenses such as vehicles for minor children). Then analyzing these expenses to determine the best feasible way for one household to convert to two while minimizing expenses and maximizing tax implications for both households simultaneously. Certified Public Accountants and Financial Analysts are skilled in this service.

11. Completing comprehensive family net worth worksheets to use in financial negotiations

The benefits of a properly prepared and family-managed mediated divorce case will far outweigh the costly pitfalls of entering into the legal arena blindly.

- Professional costs are substantially less, saving the family anywhere from $40,000 to several hundred thousand dollars in unnecessary professional fees

- The length of time in the process is greatly reduced which results in lower emotional impact on the family members

The amount of conflict between spouses is minimized therefore paving the way for a more productive and peaceful co-parenting relationship post divorce and children are especially less impacted

Even Divorce Attorneys use these methods in their own divorces. J. Richard Kulerski (40 year Divorce Attorney veteran) and Kari Cornelison stated it best in their 2/9/2012 article in the Huffington Post entitled *"What Do Divorce Lawyers Do in Their Own Divorces?"*

"They try to stay out of court...they do everything they can to settle their case before it reaches the court system. ...They resist the inclination to fight.

They think going to court is a losing proposition that wastes energy, time and money and is a last resort. They regard litigation as a counter-productive force that destroys their chances of achieving a healthy negotiation climate.

They know there are no winners in a divorce battle and that the only outcome of a divorce trial can only define the extent of how much they will lose financially.

Their experience is that everyone leaves the litigation process feeling frustrated, disillusioned and poorer. Divorce insiders know that over 90% of all cases settle before trial.

They know that feelings, emotions and immoral behaviors do not count in a courtroom and the judge is prohibited from considering these elements in reaching a decision.

They know that the emotional devastation caused by litigation can last for decades and is often irreparable."

These same sentiments are echoed by Christian Denmon, of Denmon &Denmon, Trial Attorney in his article "*What Every Divorce Lawyer Should Tell Their Clients*" (Huffington Post 3/18/15)

> *Divorce is not as cheap as you think. Divorce lawyers are notoriously terrible at helping the clients understand the full cost of a divorce at the beginning of the process...and worry that "sticker shock" from a candid assessment and a true estimated fee for legal services might send them straight out the door looking for other counsel.*
>
> *Hiring an accountant early can save you money later.*
>
> *Some attorneys milk your case....be wary of attorneys that charge only by the hour...*
>
> *See a financial planner if you stand to receive substantial assets.*
>
> *Seek emotional help when needed. Embrace the help of counselors who are trained in helping you through a difficult and emotional time. Do not rely on your attorney for emotional help. Your attorney is overpriced and under qualified to help in that regard.*

We strongly recommend you print these articles and share them with your clients. They are very thorough in explaining the pitfalls that most families cannot even imagine or foresee prior to engaging in the legal divorce process.

The Long-Term Family Value of Mediation versus Litigation

Edited by Marti Kitchens Cobb, LMFT, LPC, MA, Registered Mediator

When parties cannot negotiate an agreement through meetings or correspondence, a formal mediation by a professional registered Mediator may be helpful or necessary. There are two types of mediations and most Divorce Mediation Centers will conduct either one:

A Private Mediation

A private mediation is when the spouses take the initiative to seek out a Divorce Mediation Center or private Mediator to settle their divorce.

A Court Ordered Mediation

A court ordered mediation is when the family has already filed for divorce and the Court orders that the couple attempt mediation before the Judge will agree to the time and expense of a trial. All parties who file (even if they are "Pro Se"-

meaning representing themselves without legal representation) could be subject to a Court ordered mediation. In recent years more county court systems have adopted this mandate and fewer families require a trial as a result.

What to Expect in Mediation:

Private Mediations:

- The parties agree to mediate without a court ordered mandate

- The parties can choose their own Mediator or Divorce Mediation Center, and dates and times that are convenient to the family

- The parties can choose to mediate alone with a Mediator or have Attorneys present

- The parties can be in the same room OR separate rooms and the Mediator "shuttles" back and forth between rooms

Pro's of Private Mediation:

Choosing your own Mediator can have more productive results

It shows a willingness to work together and will be perceived as positive should the case go to litigation

It could be the final step in the process if it is successful, avoiding costs related to Court ordered conferences with the Judge and court mandated mediations

Con's of Private Mediation:

If the representing Attorneys are not present, the parties may choose to withdraw certain aspects of the agreement pending review by their Attorneys which could delay finality of the case

Court Ordered Mediations:

- A mediation that is ordered by the court, and can be limited with little flexibility on date and time of the mediation. It is similar to a court ordered appearance wherein parties must attend the ordered date and failure to do so could have repercussions. A court appointed Mediator is assigned to the case.

- For a court ordered mediation to be most effective, both party's Attorneys should attend. That way, any agreement will have the stamp of approval of the parties and their Attorneys at the close of the mediation. An agreement is signed and the need to have a Judge decide the case is eliminated. The Plaintiff's Attorney will take the agreement to a Judge for signature without the need for the parties to appear.

- The parties can be in separate rooms and the Mediator shuttles back and forth.

- When there is domestic violence in the marriage, mediation in the courthouse is required because safety provisions are made.

Pro's of a Court Ordered Mediation:

It is the best way to avoid a trial of a high conflict case

The Attorneys attend as witnesses that can support any issues that come up later

Safety features are in place in domestic violence cases

Con's of a Court Ordered Mediation:

These can be very stressful and intimidating if conducted in the Courthouse

Sometimes they are not productive with controlling parties if the assigned mediator is not skilled at containing runaway discussion. A controlling party can run up the legal fees with no intention in participating in genuine negotiation

How the Process Works

All parties start the meeting together to go over the ground rules of mediation do's and don'ts and general questions are answered and the *Guidelines for Mediation* are read and signed. An outline of the areas of mediation and goals are discussed and then the mediation process begins based on the outline established. Decisions made by the parties are documented as the mediation progresses and a *Memorandum of Understanding* is provided to an agreed upon Attorney to prepare the finalized filing documents.

* It should be noted that general filing documents do not include any additional paperwork federally required for separation of retirement accounts (401 K, IRA's, pensions) and additional documents and filings for movement of monies in these accounts requires seeking a professional who specializes in these forms with additional fees related to these filings.

Costs of Mediation

Mediator fees generally range from $200-$400 per hour. Parties are expected to share 50/50 of the total fees incurred at the mediation unless negotiated otherwise, and must pay this fee by cash or check at the closing of the mediation.

Attorney fees incurred are the hourly rate of the Attorney and are above and beyond the fees for the Mediator.

Depending on the content that needs to be resolved, mediations can take as little as 2 hours or up to 10 hours in a day. Multiple mediation days may be required if assets are complicated or there is high conflict between the parties.

Safe Guards in High Conflict or Domestic Violent couples:

When elements of domestic violence are present, a Mediator trained in domestic violence is recommended. In the case of a family violence arrest, the court requires a mediator with DV qualifications. A mediator who has also been trained in Family Violence Intervention Prevention (FVIP is a court-ordered psycho-education group approach in Georgia and other states) offers additional benefits.

In private mediations (no arrest) safety measures are taken to not leave the parties alone and allow them to depart at separate intervals. "Shuttle" style mediation is usually more effective.

In court ordered mediations, the mediation takes place in the court house and a deputy on duty is assigned to be present outside of the door of the mediation should an intervention be necessary to protect the parties

What to Bring to Mediation:

1) A complete comprehensive family net worth spreadsheet listing all of the family assets with values and current debt balances

2) A complete comprehensive family expense spreadsheet for each separate household (with realistic projections of anticipated 2nd household expenses if the couple has not yet separated). The spreadsheets should include all extracurricular, private school and medical needs for the children.

   Supporting documentation should be organized neatly in a binder with reference tabs to save time referring to them during mediation. When reference materials are not organized, a family can incur unnecessary billable hours from professionals just weeding through files or papers. The documentation should include all pre-nuptual and post nuptial agreements, all current reports of stock/bond portfolio's, corporate savings, stock options, retirement plans, 401k, pension plans, current social security statements, all banking accounts including: savings, checking, money markets, CD's, life insurance policies, itemized list of household furniture, vehicles, boats, trailers, and tangible assets, last 3 years of tax statements, all current paystubs from employers and worksheets and recommendations from an Accountant or Financial Analyst/Planner recommending settlement options if the family has chosen the alternative method of settlement and sought this advice.

3) A completed sample parenting plan prepared by each party as to their preferences for custody with the children

4) Checkbook or cash for Mediator fees and Attorney fees

We also recommend that each parent bring photographs of the children to display for themselves to remind them to put the children first should discussions get heated.

Who Benefits from Mediation and Why You Want to Recommend Your Clients Mediate:

There are so many long term benefits of mediation over litigation. Primarily it starts the spouses off on a cooperative method of resolving issues that will likely preside post the divorce settlement. Time and again couples who have chosen to litigate are continually reminded that divorce proceedings will not bring about the punishment or revenge NOR the one-sided settlement they are seeking and that actually the entire family loses greatly (great sums of money never to be recovered) and only the Attorneys win.

The value of mediation for:

The children- It shows children that their parents love them and want to work together in their best interest and it mentors a good example of how healthy people resolve differences

*Your Client-*A low conflict method means less wounding, a shorter healing period and a productive co-parenting relationship post divorce, it is simply better parenting for the child

*The Family Checkbook-*A mediated divorce final costs will average from $3,000-$7,000. A litigated divorce final costs will average from $45,000-$100,000+

Types of Trained/Registered Mediators:

Basically, there are two types of mediators: those who are professional attorneys and those who are professional therapists. Attorneys gain their training in law school learning the expertise of arguing accumulative case law to provide evidence to win in a court of law. Therapists gain their training learning how to help resolve relational issues and conflict and set healthy boundaries for lasting relationships.

There are benefits to using a Registered Therapist Mediator.

- A Therapist Mediator due to their professional education can detect behaviors of parties that are rooted in control or manipulation and have the skills to set boundaries to keep negotiations on track and moving forward toward resolution

- An Attorney Mediator whose professional education is rooted in supporting argument in debate may lack the professionally trained skills of detecting emotional control behaviors of conflict resolution which leaves parties vulnerable for run-away mediation fees and delayed resolutions

How your client can find a Mediator:

Seek Family Divorce Mediation Centers in your market with Therapist trained credentials (PhD, LMFT, LPC, and LCSW). There are also statewide online listings under "ADR-Alternative Dispute Resolution Directory", "Office of Dispute Resolution of your state or contact your state's professional "Mediators Association"

******

Most judicial districts have some sort of mediation services. They may be offered privately or through the court system. Each state has developed their own system or rules for offering a mediation process. It is good to check with the clerk of court in the county in which you are divorcing to obtain accurate information about available services in your county and state.

Preparing Clients for Abusive Tactics in Divorce

Edited by Leslie Dinkins-Perez, LCSW
Kelley Linn, Advocate

If the marital relationship has elements of control and abuse, this is a very strong indicator that the divorce process will escalate these elements; sometimes to a devastating financial and emotional level, leaving survivors with long term debt or bankrupt and with emotional wounding very difficult to overcome. Let's look at what causes abuse and the mindset of an abuser:

What Causes Abuse?
(Adapted from "*Why Does He Do That*" by Lundy Bancroft

The one and only thing that causes abuse are the choices of the abuser based on their belief system. It is truly that simple. An abuser's belief system fuels their thoughts, feelings and ultimately reinforces their choice to act based on those thoughts and feelings, and they usually act very inappropriately. We all get angry, frustrated, sad, stressed, etc. but we do not all act inappropriately despite our feelings. Abuse is a CHOICE and it is the choice of the ABUSER, not the victim. These belief systems are in no way the victims fault. An abuser isn't abusive because they are angry, they are angry because they think like an abuser. Their problem is not that they respond to conflict inappropriately, the abuse is operating *prior* to the conflict, and it usually *creates* the conflict and determines the shape that the conflict will take.

An abusers basic belief system is rooted in the following:

- Entitlement: "I have the right to _____."

- Justification: "I have the right to because _____."

- Externalization of responsibility (blame): "It's your/their fault, not my fault"

- Control: An abusers problem is not that they *lose* control of their behavior; it's that they try to *take* control of their victim

- Twisting things into their opposites: This is a crazy-making game that always makes the abuser come out on top; quite often to make the Abuser seem like the victim

- Denial and Minimization: "I didn't do that", "It's not a big deal", "What are you talking about", "That never happened" "It didn't happen like that"

- Manipulation including:

   Changing moods abruptly and frequently

   Denying the obvious about what they are doing or feeling

   Convincing the victim that what the abuser wants them to do is best for the victim

   Getting the victim and others to feel sorry for the abuser

   Getting the victim to blame themselves and others for what the abuser does

Using "confusion" tactics in arguments, such as redirecting to other topics

Lying or misleading victim and others about their actions, desires or reasons for doing things

Getting the victim and those they care about to turn on each other (often with their own children)

The desire to have unlimited, unconditional sexual access to their victim

The desire to impress others by having the victim as their partner

The desire to possess and control their victim

"Possession": "I own you"

"Objectification" and "Depersonalization" of their victim: If they own them, there is no empathy that comes with the negative effects of their abuse of them

Confusing love and abuse: what an abuser thinks of as love is defined as:

The desire to have the victim devote their life to keeping the abuser happy with no outside interference from friends, families or co-workers

The following example allows us to understand the possessive perspective of an Abuser toward their victim/target:

An abuser thinks of their target like the Abuser's car, an object that they possess.

Think of your own car. Your car's sole purpose is to sit there and wait for you to tell it what to do. It does not act on its own. If you come out to the driveway and your car is driving away, you wouldn't think it was possible for it to be acting on its own; you would think someone MUST be driving it. In addition, because it is YOUR car, you would be angry if it was driving away and do everything you could to stop that from happening because no matter how you had treated the car, it shouldn't be driving away.

Think about how you treat your car. You were really good to it when you first got it, because it was new, but the newness wore off. You could clean it, or not clean it, change the oil or not change the oil, put premium gas in it or not, keep it clean and neat, wash it or not, mess up the interior or clean it up really good sometimes if other people are going to be around it (as if you do it all the time), fix it or not fix it or only fix it enough so it will keep doing what you tell it to do.

You don't feel bad for the car if you don't take care of it. You don't worry about how the car feels or how the way you are driving it might have long-lasting negative effects on the car. If it breaks down, you get it fixed. Why? Because you need it to continue to take care of you and do everything you tell it to. You need it to be there for you. You don't worry about being there for it.

Additionally, every abuser has a specific time when they feel they finally "own" their target. Counselors will often hear "They didn't act like this until we got married." For abusers they could view the moment of ownership at the time of any of these relational thresholds:

first time they had sex
when the relationship became exclusive
when they move in together
when they got engaged

when they got married
when she got pregnant
when the baby was born
when the target became financially dependent on the abuser.

Usually a client can identify which one of these catalysts was the switch that flipped the relationship.

This is how an abuser thinks of their target, as an object they possess that they can treat however they want to. Regardless of how they are treated, the target is still supposed to sit and wait for the abuser's directions and do everything the abuser tells them to without question. This is one of the roots of entitlement and this is the thinking that fuels an abusers actions. This example can be very helpful when coaching a client who is asking "How could he/she do/think/say that?"

With this understanding of an abuser we can further explain what abusers may do during the divorce process. The behaviors we outline are an escalation of the abusers attempts to maintain control and possession when they realize these are slipping away as their partner gains independence. Many times they will escalate to a very unreasonable, toxic and even dangerous level as the finality of the impending divorce approaches. For those targets in a violent relationship, statistics have shown the first 24 months post separation and/or divorce can be the most dangerous for the target and safety measures should be taken seriously and put in place.

The forms of abuse through the judicial divorce process can cover one or all areas of known abuse including financial abuse, verbal/emotional abuse, physical abuse, legal abuse and even Divorce Attorneys can contribute to the abuse. It is not uncommon for a narcissistic personality to hire a similar personality type Attorney to represent them which adds an additional level of wounding to an already devastated relationship.

Financial Abuse includes:

- Move/hide/withhold family assets (money, vehicles, housing)

- Provide false misleading financial information for financial negotiations

- Incur additional debt under joint credit cards to damage credit ranking and create financial hardship

- Leave Spouse temporarily without financial means to provide for self and children

- Take actions to bankrupt Spouse and family (take out additional lines of credit, etc.)

How to respond to financial abuse:

- Gather and prepare financials *well in advance* of contacting an Attorney and filing for divorce so that the financial records are documented *before* the abusive spouse has the ability to manipulate, hide or move them (Transitions Divorce Prep Workbook provides a detailed method of how to do this)

- Preparing and gathering financial information in advance not only reduces the opportunity for financial abuse, but it minimizes the likelihood of an extended time in the legal process and greatly reduces the grossly exaggerated costs to recover them through legal means

Verbal/Emotional Abuse includes:

- Attack spouses character in legal documents and proceedings with the Judge

- Make false slanderous unsubstantiated claims (Attorneys can make outlandish claims that they never intend to substantiate because the law protects attorneys from libel and slander lawsuits)

- Manipulate family, friends, children, employer and court appointed officials such as Guardian ad litem and Forensic Child Psychologist with false claims and testimony

- Threaten to bankrupt family to force spouse to agree to an unfair settlement agreement

- Threaten and take actions to take custody of children away from spouse

- Alienate and isolate spouse from their support system by manipulation of children, family, friends, employer and neighbors, etc...

How to respond to Verbal/Emotional abuse:

- Prepare and help realign the client with realistic expectations of verbal and mental tactics, educate them to expect unrealistic threats and teach them with practice how not to engage in worry or combative communication with abuser; to understand that often untruths are told in court and on documents as a strategy. Help diffuse the clients response by coaching detachment techniques and practicing boundary techniques when communicating with spouse, encouraging minimal communication by utilizing email and text messages instead of live conversations

- Under advisement of an Attorney, the spouse can obtain affidavits from family, friends and co-workers as evidence to refute any false and unsubstantiated claims

- Collection of custodial diaries and logs are documented evidence to support a proposed parenting plan and also refute false and unsubstantiated claims and minimize manipulation of court appointed officials. (In civil cases court rulings are not based on what is "said" but what is actually "proved" with evidence, therefore daily logs and testimonial affidavits can far outweigh slanderous comments).

- Insistence of a speedy mediation settlement to avoid threat of bankruptcy or new debt

Physical Abuse includes:

- Threaten the safety of a spouse and/or children

- Assault the spouse or stage an altercation then call police and have spouse arrested

- Physically compromise the physical safety of a spouse

How to respond to physical abuse:

- Educate the client on the potential of manipulated staged altercations (*Hanging On By My Fingernails*-by Janie McQueen explores this trend in unethical legal strategies)

- Complete the Jacquelyn C Campbell, PhD, RN Danger Assessment and check for lethality risk

- Encourage the client to seek treatment immediately at a hospital or doctor's office where records can be established and get copies of these records post event

- Instruct the client to document wounds and bruises with eye witnesses and photographs

- Encourage the client to seek a Temporary Protective Order if physical violence has occurred

- Encourage no physical appearances of spouses together outside of required court appearances with minimal contact when possible

Legal Abuse by Spouse includes:

- Make false claims and reports to the Department of Family & Child Services to start an investigation and report in an attempt to create false evidence

- Attempt to have spouse arrested and manipulate the legal system by staging an altercation then calling police

- Going to police to file a TPO against spouse even when spouse has not been abusive

- Going to police and attempting to file an arrest warrant against spouse

How to respond to legal abuse:

Move as swiftly through the divorce process as possible, prolonged cases leave the window of opportunity open to legal abuse

How Attorneys can Contribute to the Abuse:

(Adapted and reprinted with permission from Domestic Abuse Intervention Project, 202 E. Superior Street, Duluth, MN 55802, 218-722-2781, www.theduluthmodel.org.
Shared with permission of the co-creator: P.C. Wheeler, pcwheel@earthlink.net.
Distributed by the National Center on Domestic and Sexual Violence (www.ncdsv.org)

Power and Control: Lawyer-Client Relationship

The following is information from educational materials for Attorneys citing behaviors that can be considered abusive in the lawyer-client relationship. Attorneys are guided to avoid:

Using Coercion and Threats

Making or carrying out threats to do something to harm the client, threatening to withdraw as counsel of record on the client's case, threatening to commit incompetent or unethical practice by violating the State Bar disciplinary rules of professional conduct, threatening to request the court to order a psychological evaluation of the client without just reason, ambushing and railroading the client to prevent informed decisions, exaggerating the harmful outcomes to the client, pressuring the client to accept a plea deal offer, pressuring the client to do illegal things

Using Terrorism and Assault

Making the client afraid by using looks, tones, demeanors, gestures, actions, staging temper tantrums, violating rules of politeness, rules of orderly, fair meetings and the State Bar ethics code, displaying weapons or other objects or images of violence, terrorizing the client, sadistically manipulating the client, psychologically assaulting the client

Using Emotional Abuse
Putting the client down, making the client feel bad about themselves, calling the client names, making the client think they are crazy, playing mind games, humiliating the client, making the client feel guilty

Using Isolation guilt
Isolating the client and forbidding client to consult with other lawyers without permission, using presumed guilt or suspicion of guilt of client to justify abuse, using private meetings instead of phone, mail and email communications, refusing to state the purpose of meetings

Minimizing, Denying and Blaming
Making light of the abuse and not taking client's concerns about it seriously, saying the abuse didn't happen, shifting responsibility for abusive behavior onto victim, saying the client caused the abuse

Using Information Abuse
Misrepresenting the experience and specialized knowledge of the attorney, using asymmetric information to mislead the client, preventing client from seeing all the evidence, providing insufficient information for client to make an informed decision, using misrepresentation, double-talk, stonewalling and obfuscation to prevent informed decisions, not informing the client about public access to the case file at the court house, refusing to communicate, explain and clarify in writing, failing to disclose State Bar ethics rules existence and contact information

Using Attorney Privilege
Acting like the boss, treating the client like a servant, making the big decisions, ignoring the client's instructions, decisions and best interest, failing to get client's consent, being the one to define lawyer-client roles, not writing a fee contract, preventing preview of contract before signing, making unilateral changes to contract after initial agreement, using vague, ambiguous, ineffective language that protects the lawyer but not the client, refusing arbitration

Using Economic Abuse
Making the client pay more money, not refunding client's money if not used for the stipulated purpose or if not earned, using bait-and-switch tactics after receiving advance fee payment, prolonging phone calls or meetings to increase billable charges

By the end of this process the victimized spouse is so traumatized and exhausted from abuse coming from so many sources that they will usually settle for far less than the law provides for them just to get relief from the legal process.

Importance of Mediation to Avoid Court in an Unbalanced Abusive Relationship

Abusive spouses generally lack respect for authority, therefore court ordered appearances and financial and custodial court ordered decrees and settlements hold less motivation for them to uphold than a mediated agreement that the abuser contributes to. If a controlling person has input and control over what they *agree* to do rather than what they are *ordered* to do, they are much more likely to uphold the conditions of the agreement. What good is a court ordered settlement that is ignored by an abusive ex-spouse that requires tens of thousands of dollars to enforce post trial?

We advise clients to stay out of court if at all possible. Swift mediated settlements result in less time in the process for abuse to occur. Costs are substantially less versus trials. And because of the unpredictability of the outcome of a trial, it is better for the client to avoid a trial altogether. Mediated agreements are more often followed by Abusers versus court mandates. If safety is an issue, a "shuttle" format can be used in mediation with parties in separate rooms, and safety measures taken.

Recommendations for a Client in the legal arena with an abusive partner:

> In *Splitting-Protecting Yourself while Divorcing Someone with Borderline or Narcissistic Personality Disorder-* Author, LCSW and Seasoned Divorce Attorney and Mediator, Bill Eddy quotes the

following regarding how to think and feel about legal abusive tactics in divorce:

"Manage with an assertive approach, focus your energy on what is important in your case and avoid wasting energy by overreacting unnecessarily to certain behaviors you can ignore. The assertive approach gives you energy, KEEP CALM, stop and think before you act. Think strategically, not emotionally.

Avoid being passive, but also make sure your approach is assertive without being aggressive. Aggressive tactics usually backfire in court.

What is the Assertive Approach?

Start documenting right away. High conflict divorces often start with an emergency hearing about true or false allegations of abusive behaviors, it is critical that you put together detailed, accurate information (evidence) to present to the court.

Record detailed information about parenting behaviors (yours and your spouse), only focus on actual, factual statements and behaviors and avoid opinions and interpretations.

Think strategically, not reactively or emotionally. Avoid acting out of frustration and anger. *At all times,* avoid reacting and communicating with your spouse without advice. *STOP AND THINK.* Check with your Therapist whenever you feel like communicating angrily with your partner, process the anger with your Therapist first, then seek advice from your Attorney to determine if a response is even required. It is better to process the anger in therapy rather than putting something angry in writing or in a voice mail that could inadvertently become a damaging court document. CHOOSE YOUR BATTLES, there will be many letters from your spouse or their Attorney that can be very provocative but don't always require a response.

Expose Abusers behavior with evidence: voicemails or emails and witnesses of events.

What evidence are you looking for?

-*False statements*-prepare evidence that proves the statements are false, exaggerated or misrepresented

-*Patterns of Abuse*

-*Truth about you (with affidavits, and documentation)*

(One form of evidence is letters or cards from the Spouse documenting good parenting skills like Mother's Day or Father's Day cards)

If the assertive approach is taken *early in the case*, the Abuser will usually back off, give up or target someone else.

Don't make yourself a target

When in a family court battle, you need to be as perfect as possible. Any public and/or private actions may be exposed and twisted around to fit their adversarial purposes. Social media presence in a conservative positive light is very important.

Keep a low profile on the Internet (temporarily discontinuing social networking pages which are often used in court as evidence of bad behavior)

Stop and think about parenting decisions

Be very honest-admit your own errors and poor judgment as soon as possible to your Attorney in order for them to be prepared for a response

Manage your own emotions and do not engage in escalated behavior. Practice responding in a matter-of-fact way and getting out of the interaction as quickly as possible. Some effective responses include:

> *"That's interesting, I'll think about that"*
> *"I'll give that some thought and get back to you in 2 days"*
> *"Give me time to consider this and will get back to you"*
> *"I'm sorry you feel that way, I will take that into consideration"*

*Develop patience and flexibility (work on this in therapy with roll-playing)

*Do not send hostile e-mails to anyone or leave hostile voice messages for anyone

*Avoid Forensic Psychological Assessments and appointments of a Guardian Ad Litem, they risk manipulation by a spouse that is skilled in deceptions and are extremely costly (ranging from an additional $10,000 to $75,000) and rarely produce the outcome victims anticipate."

Sometimes the best approach is to work on acceptance of the court's orders in therapy. You may be absolutely correct that the orders were bad, that the court completely misunderstood your case, but sometimes nothing can be done. This is the time to focus on doing the best you can with the situation. Make the most of your time with your children, your positive influence may outweigh the harm you fear the other parent will do.

- Expect the high conflict to remain years after the divorce.

- Avoid being too close to the ex-spouse.

- Avoid being too rejecting of the ex-spouse

- Deal with ex-spouse at arm's length.

- Expect new battles and *keep good records* of parenting problems, confrontations and visitation-exchange behavior. Some of the worst legal custody battles occur after the divorce is actually over. The apparent catalyst in many of these cases is the request to reduce child support. The best defense against such a post divorce battle is to continue to keep records on parenting behavior and to have other people witness that the child is doing well with you. Photos and videotapes of good times together with you and the children help block new allegations.

The Importance of Continued Therapy through and Post Divorce

Edited by Leslie Dinkins-Perez, LCSW
Kelley Linn, Advocate

Many clients will feel that once the family has filed for divorce it is the "end" of their troubles when in fact the divorce filing is actually the beginning of what can be a very challenging experience. As discussed in earlier chapters giving your clients a very clear perspective of realistic expectations can greatly improve their resiliency through the legal process.

We tell our clients it will definitely get worse before it gets better. Until the divorce settlement is finalized by an order from a Judge, all of the impending issues of financial independence and child visitation leave your client stuck in a void of unknowing what their "new-normal" will look like. During the process and well after the settlement your client will need help processing the changes taking place. As with any major change in life the death of the "happily-ever-after" dream brings with it traditional grieving associated with any substantial loss.

Another one of the key concerns most new divorcees experience is the isolation caused by the change in their family structure. Having been one half of a couple for many years, being single again can be a frightening or lonely prospect. Support groups are an excellent way for them to acknowledge, share and validate common emotions of grieving and change that are related to the divorce process.

While most support groups are member driven and are simply a sharing arena for one to vent about their ex-spouse, we encourage instead a structured, professionally led processing group that can focus on processing grief but also encourage healing as well.

With the assistance of seasoned licensed professional counselors, Transitions Resource has published two support group program workbooks (available on Amazon.com). The *Transitions Recover/Discover Workbook* and *Transitions Recover/Discover in God's Word Workbook* (for faith-based practitioners) that are fourteen week session agendas for practitioners.

The structure allows the participant to journal, share and experiment with techniques that will help them springboard into an emotionally healthy new season of life. Facilitators need not have personally experienced divorce to be effective, because the program focuses on processing grief of loss and recovery of self esteem, confidence, hope and joy, skills which practitioners already have.

The Recover/Discover programs can be used one- on-one in private sessions or in a group setting. Leading a support group is also an excellent tool for practitioners to identify danger signs or trouble spots of certain participants who might need alternative support or additional processing or in-depth therapies outside of the group setting. Because a structured processing group involves group therapy, facilitators usually charge fees for participants.

A new divorcee greatly benefits from a structured group as it minimizes the isolation and shortens the mourning process. One who does not proactively seek to process this change properly can endure years of unhealthy emotional perspectives which can have a negative domino effect on children, friends and family.

What and How do Divorcees Grieve?

A divorcee can be in *denial* and *disbelief* and reluctant to believe that a spouse cheated, abused them, is addicted, or whatever the root of the relational affliction is and believes they can still change their spouse.

A divorcee may still be trying to *reason* and *bargain* to repair a permanently broken partnership "Why did they...?" "If I had only..."

A divorcee may be stuck in *anger* or *sadness* from recognition of deceptions and secrets; from realization of the loss of the "happily ever after" dream; from a violation of their own expectations; a violation of their own personal morals and ethics; from an unexpected forced change in lifestyle and/or the shortcomings of a disappointing legal outcome.

A divorcee may be *fearful* and *anxious* of the uncertainty of their future finances, future relationships, the loss of intimacy and especially the loss of control of how their children are doing when they are not with them.

How Do Divorcees Heal?

Divorce is no different than any other great loss. We have found that divorcees that heal the quickest devote time to the following practices:

1) Acknowledging their grief, feeling the pain of loss and change and proactively working through this with the proper support

2) Develop their spiritual awareness and faith that establishes hope for the future

3) Proactively reprogram their thoughts, words and actions with optimistic approaches

4) Use their experience to help others

Words of Wisdom for the Newly Divorced:

You know you are on the road to recovery and rebuilding your life when you:

- understand and manage your feelings

- use your time away from your children to focus on yourself

- invest time and energy in personal growth

- enjoy independence

- set goals for your life

- have a support system of family and friends

- realize you have the power through love and understanding to provide your child all they need to be happy and healthy

- forgive yourself and your ex-spouse

- focus on positive thoughts and beliefs for your future

- don't expect perfection from yourself or others but view all life experiences as lessons for wisdom to pass on to your children and others

Minimizing Child Wounding of Divorce

Edited by Marti Kitchens-Cobb, LPC, LMFT

All children need to experience their childhood fully. They need to love and to feel loved and supported by both parents. They need to feel safe, both physically and emotionally.

All children of divorce experience their parents' conflict. They worry about who will take care of them, they fear the loss of one or both of their parents, experience loyalty conflicts, often blame themselves for the divorce, experience feelings of mad, sad, scared and lonely and have fantasies of their parents getting back together. With divorce children feel the loss of their sense of family, security, the loss of one parent or even both parents and the loss of the known, predictable familiar routine of life as they know it.

STRESSORS FOR KIDS	HOW PARENTS CAN HELP
Parental Conflict	*Develop skills for conflict management* *Stay alert and aware of how kids are hurt*
Divided loyalties	*Acknowledge and encourage the relationship with other parent*
Feeling caught in the middle	*Don't use kids as messengers, spies or pawns* *Don't ask kids to choose between parents*
Too many changes too soon	*Minimize the number of changes (school, home, community) give time for adjustment*
Worry about their parents	*Parents seek support from adults, not their kids*
Feeling responsible	*Communicate and reassure it's not their fault, they didn't cause it and cannot fix it*
Loss of contact with one/both parent	*Have a parenting plan and stick to it* *Be there, be on time*
Transitions between homes	*Have kids ready; allow them to take toys, clothes, transition objects*
New relationships/parental dating/marriage	*Separate parental needs from kids needs* *Be aware that dating causes stress for kids* *Have empathy for the kids and allow time for them to grieve both the divorce and any new family*

Trauma and Attachment

Research shows attachments can change and can be with more than one person. Divorce can be traumatic for children, but a high conflict marriage can be even more traumatizing. Attachment buffers the impact of the trauma. Positive parenting and secure attachments to *both* parents during and after divorce are factors that significantly increase the likelihood that children will adjust and cope well with the changes.

What Children Need

Children need to have secure attachments to both parents in a stable and safe environment. They need to be allowed to express love for both parents and remain connected to both parent's lives and extended families. They need to be "allowed" to be a child, not an adult or parent confidant; deserve to be loved unconditionally and allowed to express their feelings as a child. They have the right to be informed of family changes (such as moving homes, schools, etc.). And children will fare more resiliently when their primary caregiver is reliable, predictable, consistent and nurturing to meet their needs more often than not. Consistent contact with a competent noncustodial parent has been shown to enhance the adjustment of children, especially children of the same sex of the noncustodial parent.

Children's Stages of Grieving Divorce-Similar to Kubler-Ross model

- *Denial*: simply do not believe their parents are going to divorce, they reassure themselves that their parents will stay together, reconcile or soon reunite, this often persists for years

- *Anger*: are furious at parents for allowing it to happen, ruining their lives and often some form of acting out accompanies this anger

- *Bargaining*: they may believe some real or imagined misbehavior on their part drove the parents apart and may try to undo the damage by changing their own actions

- *Depression*: experience pervasive sadness, unusually tired, express physical pain Often self-motivated children who reach this stage need be watched closely as they may be overcompensating to control the suffering and emotions they feel

- *Acceptance*: occurs mostly in older children and young adults as they gain the emotional experience to understand that the divorce was for the best

Parents experience stages too. They might inadvertently put the emotional needs of their children on hold while they deal with their own feelings. Children suffer as a result and may become stuck in one of the stages, often the denial stage. Consequences of the divorce are often considerable for one or both parents. Emotional, physical and financial consequences often affect their parenting skills. They may elevate the child to a role of companion or may become harsh or distant as they direct hostility for the other parent onto the children. The children may be unsupervised for long periods of time (might be viewed as abandonment) older siblings may be overburdened with watching younger siblings or added house chores.

What Children Don't Need

Kids should never be put in the position of being a message carrier, family spy or interrogated after a visit with the other parent. They should never be told negative information about either parent, exposed to the conflict between parents or burdened with adult issues such as dating or finances. They should never be used as a weapon or as leverage against the other parent.

High conflict divorces can be traumatic for children and parents. Trauma disrupts attachment and can result in regression and other behavioral changes in children.
Parents need to remain emotionally engaged with their children and avoid withdrawing from them. Parents need to be aware of their hostile feelings and behaviors they show to each other and take measures to ensure that this hostility is not directed at their children as misdirected emotions. Sometimes, a child may physically or behaviorally resemble the hated

spouse and serve as a substitute target. Therapists can help parents recognize this harmful tendency.

We know that parental conflict is the biggest predictor for a poor outcome for children. Children will act out, turn inward and withdraw, display poor social skills, have low self esteem and set poor boundaries with themselves and others. They may choose poor relationships when they mature. Prolonged stress hormones in children can actually change brain functioning that can cause symptoms that can mimic ADHD.

Here is an exercise that can be used with a Co-Parent Client:

"Do this the next time you are about to get into an argument with the other parent:

Picture your child in your mind or look at a picture and say to yourself, "I know that what I am about to do is damaging to you and is likely to affect you forever. But right now, indulging my anger is more important than your well being."

What will your choice be?

Developmental Stages

What Infants Experience 0-18 Months

Infants are learning how to trust people and to learn what it means to be part of a family. Despite assumptions, infants are affected by conflict. They commonly show signs of distress when exposed to parents who are arguing, who are unable to provide adequate care, or when schedules are changed. These signs include fussiness, agitation, nervousness, crying, listlessness (disinterest), and regression in already learned skills. They may become delayed in developmental milestones and may develop separation anxiety.

Guide parents to maintain a consistent routine for your child focused on frequent (daily if possible) love and affection from each parent. Parents should provide frequent parenting time with each parent and visits should be designed not to disrupt the stable daily routine.

0-3 years is a critical window for child development. The brain is developing (or not) based on the child's interaction with his/her environment. The foundation is being laid for future emotional regulation, the ability to pay attention, to learn and develop empathy.
Newborns are dependent on their parents longer than any other species. Dependency spawns fear of abandonment; when one parent leaves, children can feel rejected therefore keeping the noncustodial parent (often the father) involved is *very* important.

What Toddlers Experience 19 Months – 3 Years

Toddlers are learning to be a unique, separate person while seeking parent approval. Toddlers are aware of their parents fighting and they may act out or try to get the parents to stop. They may feel unsafe and stressed when a parent is unable to take care of them. They might believe they are the cause of the problems. At this stage, routine and predictability provide security for them. They may become uneasy, stressed, and afraid without routine. Signs of distress include regression in milestone development behavior or withdrawal. When normal patterns of sleeping and eating change they may develop fears. Most toddlers require security objects.

What Preschoolers Experience (3-5 years old)

Preschoolers are learning new skills, developing their own personality and independence. They may believe they are the cause of the divorce (magical egocentric thinking) and don't understand the parental conflicts. They may become frightened and confused by immense changes and have a fear of abandonment. They may fear they will never see the parent who moved out of the home. They may try to magically think the divorce away and think their parents will get back together. Signs of distress include saying things that might indicate they feel responsible for the conflict and divorce. They may become clingy, regress, be bossy or try to control everything, display increased anger and aggression, withdraw, may worry about the other parent they are not with (early signs of parentified behavior), display low self esteem, or depression, or start to have nightmares. Their fear of abandonment is more concrete- "if one parent leaves, will the other leave too?" Or "If Mommy and Daddy stopped loving each other will they stop loving me too?"

To minimize acting out (clinging, tantrums) consider having a plan for transitioning from one parent to the other if switching parents is difficult for the child. For example, perhaps one parent can drop the child off at school and the other picks up. Provide predictable, consistent routines and reassure the child they will be back at a specific time when they leave and follow through with the promise consistently. Parents should continually reassure them that their love for them will never change, that they are safe and will always be taken care of. Parents can provide opportunities for children to express their feelings and validate those feelings, example: "I know you feel sad right now. This is very hard for you." Parents should keep each other informed about special events in the child's life and both should attend. Parents should inform teachers and childcare providers of changes in their family so that they can provide extra support and watch for signs of distress.

Family is very important at this age. Family wholeness is where children find security to successfully venture out and develop their self-esteem and identity. They may have strong feelings of sadness, anger, guilt, loneliness and grieve for the loss of family as they know it (but also grieve for loss of friends, neighborhood, school, pets, church, extended family). They will miss the other parent when they aren't together or may force parental interaction in any way they can. They may have difficulty concentrating in school. They also may fear that one parent will stop loving them.

Peer relationships are also becoming very important as the child is learning to master social skills and rules, express feelings and master cognitive and academic skills. Self esteem grows when they function well with peers and family. Children thrive on structure and routine. They prefer play, so play therapy is the most effective form at this age. They also often have different relationships with each parent at this age, preferring their mother for some things and father for others. They may feel responsible for the divorce and egocentrism is still present at this age. They may side with one parent, usually the one that is the neediest which it is why it is important to emphasize to clients that they need to care well for themselves. Some children will try to protect a parent and feel the need to take care of them. They may try to provide emotional support for a parent who is suffering. Signs of distress include changes in grades or attitude, withdrawal, frequent crying, acting sad, increase in physical symptoms (headaches or stomachaches), lack of enthusiasm, acting out, emotional dysregulation or sleep problems.

At this age they are at high risk of parentification which is role reversal where a child's personal needs are sacrificed in order to take care of the emotional and psychological needs of the parent. The child becomes the parent's confidant and is brought up to and interacted with on a peer level by the adult. Often, the child may become aligned with one parent against the other.

The child responds to the emotional needs of the parent or sibling and can act as a peacemaker, confidant, or do actual care giving tasks such as preparing meals, doing household chores, handling bills and financial matters, and monitoring and caring for siblings.

Parentification is a form of child neglect. It interferes with child development, resulting in poor relationships, and poor differentiation of self from the family of origin.
Through the lens of attachment theory, parentification creates an internal working model where others are not available or cannot be trusted to respond or support or comfort in times of distress. Negative cognition is "I am not worthy or deserving of comfort or support."

A parent should accept the child's feelings and be available to listen. They should never say demeaning things about the other parent in front of the child. Parents should role model self care. They should let the child know they want them to love and spend time with the other parent and help the child see that the family is still a family, simply a different structure. Display love to the child with words AND actions and keep the other parent involved with the child as much as possible.

What Upper Elementary / Middle School Children Experience (9-12 years old)

Children at this age are learning to become more independent. They want things to be black and white and may need parents to help them make sense of things. Some children may feel the need to please their primary caregivers and therefore may have a conflict with the other parent. This can also lead to contradictory behavior with parents and conflicting loyalties. This also leads to conflict over what they want for themselves and others. They most likely will feel anger-usually directed at one parent for "messing up my life" and feel ashamed or embarrassed by any public display of parental disagreement. At this age they often worry about their parents and feel a tremendous responsibility for their well-being.

Signs of distress include aggression or acting as if divorce is of no consequence to them. Boys are more likely to have poor school performance, act out and fight, whereas girls are more likely to want to please and increase in their physical symptoms (they may have premature sexual activity usually associated with wanting to be loved). They may take on an adult role in the family and feel guilt over siding with one parent or feel angry when forced to choose one parent over another.

At this age, the parent's ability to model self care and remain in the adult role is crucial.
Parents should encourage children to be physically active to have an outlet. They should spend extra care in staying aware of what is going on with school and friends, even making school counselors aware of what is happening at home. Parents should talk with the child about feelings and what is happening and encourage them to talk with someone other than the parents to help facilitate discussions. Even six to twelve sessions with a child therapist is extraordinarily helpful at this age to allow a healthy venting with a non-biased third party. It is also especially important to never have parents speak negatively about each other and to create an environment where the child is allowed to be a child.

What Teenagers Experience (ages 13-18)

Teens are getting ready to leave home and live responsibly. They may feel anxious about leaving home and worry about their future plans and having money. They could feel responsible and guilty for the divorce. They may feel rejected or neglected and may believe the parent who moved away no longer loves them. They may resent their parents for "messing up their life" or be embarrassed or ashamed about the divorce. At this age they are also vulnerable to parentification and may feel frightened or burdened by their parents neediness.

Normal behavior of all teens includes opposition to parents and a negative attitude. They may be rebellious as a way of forging a separate identification, be extremely negative or critical and even avoid both parents. They are moody and emotionally reactive at times and self centered. Healthy teens develop self confidence and strong friendships.

A parentified child at this age can result from inappropriate expectations placed on an opposite gender child and labeling them the "man of the house now that your Dad isn't here" or a substitute "Mommy" or "Girlfriend". As a result they may be desperate to leave home sooner than planned OR talk of delaying their own plans (college or job) so they can be at home to help out. One reason they may fear leaving home is they may be concerned that if they leave, there may be no home to come back to. They may act out with increased aggression, moderate to severe legal or school problems (running away, drug or alcohol use, withdrawal, self injurious behavior) or increased sexual behavior.

Parents should model self care, let teens be teens and especially don't confuse teens with adults. Parents should offer love, support and encouragement for the teen to continue to strive for their own life goals (school or job). They should remain in a consistent parental role by setting clear expectations and boundaries for the child. Allow the teen to know and love the other parent and remain flexible regarding custody and visitation as teens often want to switch homes (making custody and support arrangements challenging). Parents should not take it personally if a teen chooses to spend more time with the opposite parent; especially the same sex parent as usually preferred and allows them input into the parenting schedule. Often, teens are busy with their own life and may not require as much visitation time but parents need to remain involved to help curtail acting out. Parents should tell their teen often that they love them and give them ample opportunities to express how they feel by giving them permission to talk openly without judgment, blame or becoming defensive.

As a side note parents should be discreet about their own dating and sexual activities.

Children's Bill of Rights:

Parents are concerned about their own rights when divorcing and mediate or go to court to protect their rights. Adults often confuse their rights with their children's rights. Encourage parents to commit to respecting their children's rights during and post divorce to ensure healthy, emotional stability and resiliency in adjusting to the changes.

As a child, I have the right to:

- *Have my parents talk to me about divorce without blaming the other parent*
- *Know the truth about the divorce and be given simple explanations*
- *Be protected from parent warfare*
- *Receive love, guidance, patience, understanding and limits*
- *Be free from having to choose one parent over the other*
- *Be free from having to be the parent or taking over adult responsibilities*
- *Be free to have all my feelings without being put down or shamed*
- *Develop and maintain independent relationships with each parent*
- *Have a physically and emotionally safe environment*
- *Maintain relationships with extended family on both sides*
- *Be financially supported by my parents regardless of how much time I spend with each parent*
- *Be reassured that the divorce is not my fault*
- *Avoid being told all the painful details of legal proceedings*
- *Avoid being made to feel guilty for loving both of my parents and want to spend time with them*
- *Avoid being asked to make custody and visitation decisions*
- *Expect both of my parents to follow the parenting plan and keep their promises*
- *Be free to concentrate on my school work, my friends and activities so I can learn and grow*
- *Not be asked to keep secrets from either parent*
- *Be a kid*

Talking to Children About Divorce

Children experience intense emotions, but they often do not understand their feelings nor do they have the words to describe what they are feeling. This confusion and frustration can show itself in children's behavior that result from their inability to manage what they are feeling. Understanding and having ways to express what it means to be happy, sad, mad, scared and lonely are essential for their development. Separation and divorce does indeed affect children. It is important for parents to have knowledge of how this change affects their children and to have the wisdom to be one of the most significant adults who make this transition result in a personal growth for them rather than a trauma and loss that is never resolved.

When parents divorce children may experience intense feelings of worry, anger, grief, resentment and hopelessness. They may doubt their parents love for them or their own self worth. Emotions are a jumbled mess. It is up to caring adults to help the child to recognize, verbalize and express their feelings to provide reassurance that it is okay to feel all these things. Feelings need to be identified, explored and openly shared and expressed in constructive ways.

How to Tell the Children

Once parents have made the decision to divorce, they should talk with each other and make a plan for what they would like to share with the children. They must take time to consider their children's feelings and needs. Spouses can often times have different priorities and may have to put their children's needs before their own for this very important discussion. It is important to tell all children together in a family environment as it sets the tone that parents plan to work together on the children's behalf.

Things to consider *together* before parents tell the children:

What will we tell the child?
Where will the child live?
Where will the parents live?
When will the parents move to new homes?
When will they see the parents and what the visitation plan will be?
How to avoid blaming each other
How to take responsibility that the decision to divorce is based on mutual problems in the relationship
How to avoid being critical of the other parent
Be prepared for questions and work out responses in advance

When Parents Tell the Children

Both parents should tell all of the children together at the same time if they can do so without volatility, blaming each other or defending themselves. A professional can coach parents and help them practice and prepare for this discussion. It is a very important discussion and should be delivered in the proper way. Timing of this discussion is also very important. Children should be told no more than 2 weeks before one parent moves out of the home. If they are told too far in advance and the change doesn't take effect, it can create false hopes of reconciliation for the children which can be confusing. Two weeks can give the children just enough time to let the news settle in before the change.

Use statements like:

- *This is a decision we have both made together*
- *We both have worked hard to stay together but we will not be able to*
- *We will get along better and be better parents to you if we live in separate homes*
- *We are getting separated and divorced*
- *Parents do not divorce children, we are not divorcing you*
- *The marriage is coming to an end, but we both will always be your parents*
- *The divorce is not your fault, you had nothing to do with the decision*
- *We both still love you, always will*
- *We will both still take care of you and spend time with you*
- *We will keep as many things the same as we possibly can (school, neighborhood, friends, etc.)*
- *We will both work together to help you through this change*
- *We are sad, and you likely will feel sad and upset and that is ok and we will help you to feel better*

Children want to know how the divorce will affect them. Children need to spend parenting time with both parents, so describe in as much detail as possible the plan for spending time with each parent. Do not allow children to dictate the terms nor encourage them to decide when or if they are going to see the other parent.

Preparing for Tough Questions:

Common questions asked by children, their interpretation and appropriate answers include:

Q: Why did you stop loving Mommy/Daddy?

This actually means "If you could stop loving each other, will you stop loving me?"
They need reassurance that your love for the children will never change

Q: *Will you ever get back together?*

Most children fantasize about their parents getting back together. Sometimes they think they can make this happen. Tell them clearly that you are not getting back together again. Let them know you understand their feelings, but it isn't going to happen.

Q: *Why did you break up our family?*

Be honest without giving too much information or placing all the blame on one parent

Q: *Do I have to go to Mom's/Dad's?*
Yes, in order for healthy development children need time with both parents.
Do not ask them to decide. Work together to resolve issues that are bothering them.

Q: *Am I getting a new Mom/Dad?*

No, parents are not replaceable. They need both of their parents. It is critical that each parent respect the child's love for the other parent. They should never try to insert a new partner into the role of Mom or Dad. New partners can easily step into the roles of friend, coach, step-parent, or bonus mentor.

Q: *Where will I live?*

Parents should know and decide the living arrangements and parenting schedules ahead of time. Children should be given a chance to explore and get a feel for the new arrangements. Parent should make the new home comfortable and inviting for the children and try to have a private place for them at each home.

Other helpful tips:
- Provide an ongoing series of talks. Once is not enough.
- Ask them what divorce means and correct misconceptions.
- Describe a plan for spending time with each parent.
- Plan to talk in a few days and be available to your children.
- You don't have to know all the answers and it is fine to admit it to them
- Make sure your motives are honorable and you are making decisions in the best interest of your children
- Make transitions between parents easy and positive.
- Children need to be reassured that both parents love them and are going to be available. They need to be told they can continue to love everyone in the family.

Q: What if my co-parent does not want to see or communicate with our child?

Your child needs to know that his other parent's failure to remain involved has nothing to do with him or how loveable he is. You must also explain in a way that does not place the other parent in a bad light no matter how angry you are at them for disengaging. This is very important to your child's self esteem. Tell them "I know you are sad and confused about why you don't see (Mommy/Daddy) anymore. He/she is having a hard time right now and I hope he/she will be able to see you soon."

Q: What if my co-parent refuses to have any communication with me?

The best way to repair lost communication is to continue to communicate as though the other person will respond. Continue to offer information about the children on a regular and timely basis and always be considerate and polite even if the response is silence or anger. You might write a message to them acknowledging what you think the problem is and how they must feel, then suggest a way to overcome it and move on. "I know you are angry at me for going through with this divorce and may not like me very much anymore. Could we find a way to talk about the children's welfare? Perhaps we could speak briefly by phone once a week to share information such as homework, sports schedules and special plans, what do you think?"

Q: Should I hide my sadness from my child? How do I handle my emotions in front of them?

Sadness is a real emotion that your child is feeling as well. Acknowledge it, explain why you are sad and include their feelings in the communication. "I'm really sad about the changes that have happened; I bet that you feel pretty sad too. Sometimes when I am sad I cry, talk to a friend or busy myself with a hobby, then after an hour or so I feel better. What works for you when you are sad?" Don't hesitate to seek professional help as you work through your grief. Your children need to know that you will be able to take care of them as well as yourself.

Q: What if my child says they don't want to see the other parent?

It is very important to encourage your child to have contact with both parents for healthy emotional development. Most children become weary of transferring houses and rebel at some point. Find out the reason they don't want to go and address it with your co-parent.

Q: How do I respond when my child tells me about my co-parent's latest romance?

Getting on with life is an important part of re-stabilizing post divorce. Any person who becomes a routine part of your child's life will become important to them and they will talk about them to make sure it is ok with you that they like them. Children deal with loyalty conflicts surrounding parent's other romances because they prefer not to incorporate another person into the picture. It's important to listen to what they have to say because you may learn about an issue that you need to address with the co-parent. If they begin to say unkind things about the other person you may want to tell them "I know it is hard to adjust to a new person in (mommy/daddy)'s life because they probably do things differently and that seems strange to you. Could you be afraid that they may take my place or you would be expected to like (him/her) more than you want to?" This will give the child permission to approach the situation at his own pace.

Q: Does counseling or bringing up the divorce make it worse, should we just not talk about it?

Talking about the divorce is critical to successful healing. It is helpful to have many conversations about it over the years. Working through it is painful; however avoiding it only prolongs healing. As children grow older they will have more in depth questions about how and why the divorce happened. Address the questions with seriousness and respect.

Q: What if my co-parent drinks/uses drugs and I don't feel safe letting the children be with them?

If there is a history of treatment you can offer proof that spending time with this parent is dangerous for the child. You may seek legal counsel regarding pursuing supervised visitation until such time as that parent can exhibit adequate parenting skills. If you are mediating the divorce, tell the mediator in private caucus and have them include a general parenting class or require medical treatment if necessary. Tell your co-parent "I am concerned about your use of _____ while you have our child in your care. I want us to help one another to be the best parents we can be, and I think some attention to this issue would be a good start. I have the name of someone who can guide us." Although you no longer must live with the substance abuse, it is in the child's best interest to help the other parent get help.

Therapy Considerations with Children

Place children into "family-in-transition" counseling immediately after the suit is filed if your family budget allows this. This important step will help your children understand the changes in your family, give them a healthy perspective on the changes as well as an outlet to vent frustrations or concerns. Six to twelve sessions with a child therapist who specializes in this area is an excellent investment to help prevent behavioral issues in the future.

Implications for Therapists

- Consider counseling at the first sign of regression or behavioral changes
- Respect the child's privacy and confidentiality in therapy
- Involve both parents in therapy if possible and educate them about children's needs and the importance of healthy co-parenting.
- Educate parents about the effects of the conflict on their children

- Guide parents in seeing the value in attending to the needs of their children, encourage them to continue to set limits, enforce bedtimes and assign chores.
- Counseling both parents and children before the divorce is believed to help in the transition at the time of separation.
- Group therapy focusing on divorce has shown to be consistently effective in studies.
- Resolving conflicts between the two parents is the greatest stress reducer in divorce for parents and children.
- An online resource for divorced parents offers co-parenting tools and regular helpful education through newsletters: www.ourfamilywizard.com

The Importance of a Comprehensive Parenting Plan

Even when there is little or no conflict between spouses it is especially beneficial to have a comprehensive parenting plan contract in place. This eliminates confusion should a conflict arise down the road. Parents don't necessarily have to follow the parenting plan word-for-word if they remain flexible, however should circumstances change, it is a solid plan they can fall back on to avoid unnecessary litigation.

Components of an Effective Parenting Plan include:

A schedule that is clear with specific dates, times, locations of pick-up and drop-off for the week, month and years

A description of who will be responsible when a parent is unavailable during their designated parenting time with children, what arrangements will be agreed upon including "first right of refusal", a baby sitter or leaving children with relatives

A transportation agreement as to who will transport children to and from co-parents

A clause on how the co-parents will manage disputes

Details on who pays and how the financial needs of the child will be met

How decisions for the child regarding education, medical needs, extracurricular activities and religion will be made

An ultimate decision making clause when parents disagree

Recommended Parenting Plans by Age of Children

Infants-Toddlers (0-3 years old)

Children up to 18 months must have security and stability in relationships. Ability to adjust to separation from one parent to be with the other can be well tolerated provided both parents have been equally involved in primary caregiver tasks. If not, it is recommended that separation from the primary caregiver be slowly incorporated into the post divorce parenting plan such as frequent, short visits by the non-primary parent with no overnight stays for six months to a year until the child can feel comfortable and secure with extended absences from the primary caregiver.

Preschoolers (4-5 years old)

Routine, predictability, structure and consistent discipline in each home are crucial at this age. Children over the age of 3 can usually tolerate overnights with both parents. This age group adjusts better to larger blocks of time with each parent so they can "settle in" to the home they are in. They will react to frequent transitions. At this age they still need a "primary" home, especially if there was one primary caregiver before the divorce. Work out a plan for the non-primary parent to become more involved so that over time the child feels equally comfortable at both homes. Plan to share information about medical, social, educational, eating and sleeping between co-parents. Develop the habit of keeping each other fully informed.

School Age (6-12 years old)

Consistent and structured co-parenting is important at this age. Because of their busy social and extracurricular activities, it will take co-parents added attention to detail to manage activities with two households. Frequent communication between parents is a key. Children will need to know where they will be, who is getting them to their activities and that both parents will be present at their extracurricular games, etc. Setting a firm weekly schedule and sticking with it provides the most consistency and minimizes confusion. It allows the children to have solid expectations. The most effective parenting plans include anywhere from 35-50% of their time spent with each parent (assuming parents don't live great distances apart). As the child increases in social skills, exposure to both male and female role models is extremely important. They will be observing parents and learning how to resolve conflict at this age.

Adolescents (13-18 years old)

Adolescents will want a say in the parenting plan and their visitation with each parent. A child may prefer more time at one home than another, usually to avoid confusion for their friends and maximize convenience for himself. It is important to keep consistent rules in both households such as curfews, telephone/computer time, acceptable activities and friends so that he does not choose one household over another. Allowing a teen to develop a healthy separation from the family is good but there needs to be some parental expectations that are met, even if the teen shows resistance. Examples would be spending at least one night a week with each parent alone, so they can keep track of the child's activities, friends and developing identity. Teens think they are ready to manage their own lives long before most of them really are. They need guidance, firm rules and consistent consequences for breaking the rules. When there are two households teens can become very manipulative if parents don't talk openly, often and provide consistent discipline with consequences.

Note that you may have more than one child and since recommendations vary among ages, parenting schedules may differ. It is important to adjust schedules as the children age. Close proximity of parents to each other is also very crucial. When one parent moves far away a child may feel alienated from that parent and the likelihood of continuing maximum advisable time with that parent may diminish as long driving times to pick up and drop off hinder ease of transfer. The best scenario is co-parent homes 15 to 20 minutes apart from each other and in the child's same school district when possible to enhance parents ability to remain involved in all activities, school conferences and after school or evening time on the spur of the moment.

SAMPLE PARENTING PLAN

This document is not to be construed as legal advice. Seek a Licensed Attorney in your state to provide an appropriate document for your case. This is only a general example of what a parenting plan would include.

Petitioner: _____

Respondent: _____

Civil Action # _____

PARENTING PLAN

☐ the parties have agreed to the terms of this plan and this information has been furnished by both parties to meet the requirements of OCGA §19-9-1. The parties agree on the terms of the plan and affirm the accuracy of the information provided, as shown by their signatures at the end of this Order.

☐ This plan has been prepared by the Judge.
This plan
☐ is a new plan
☐ modifies an existing Parenting Plan dated _____.
☐ modifies an existing Order dated _____.

CHILD'S NAME	BIRTHDATE
_____	_____
_____	_____

I. CUSTODY AND DECISION MAKING

A. LEGAL CUSTODY (choose one):

☐ with the mother
☐ with the father
☐ joint custody

B. PRIMARY PHYSICAL CUSTODY

NAME	BIRTHDATE	MOTHER	FATHER	JOINT
_____	_____	☐	☐	☐
_____	_____	☐	☐	☐

WHERE JOINT PHYSICAL CUSTODY IS CHOSEN BY THE PARENTS OR ORDERED BY THE COURT, A DETAILED PLAN OF THE LIVING ARRANGEMENTS OF THE CHILD(REN) SHALL BE ATTACHED AND MADE A PART OF THIS PARENTING PLAN.

C. DAY TO DAY DECISIONS

Each parent shall make decisions regarding day to day care of a child while the child is residing with the parent, including any emergency decisions affecting the health or safety of a child.

D. MAJOR DECISIONS

Major decisions regarding each child shall be made as follows:

Education	□ mother	□ father	□ joint
Non-emergency health care	□ mother	□ father	□ joint
Religious upbringing	□ mother	□ father	□ joint
Extracurricular activities	□ mother	□ father	□ joint
Psychological decisions	□ mother	□ father	□ joint
_____	□ mother	□ father	□ joint

E. DISAGREEMENTS

Where parents have elected joint decision making in Section I. D. above, please explain how any disagreements in decision making will be resolved, i.e., explain the process parents will use when a tie breaker is needed.

_____

_____

II. PARENTING TIME/VISITATION SCHEDULES

A. Parenting Time/Visitation

During the term of this Parenting Plan the non-custodial parent shall have at a minimum the following rights of parenting time/visitation (choose an item):

□ The weekend of the first and third Friday of each month
□ The weekend of the first, third, and fifth Friday of each month
□ The weekend of the second and fourth Friday of each month.
□ Every other weekend starting on _____.
□ Each _____ starting at _____am/pm and ending at _____ am/pm
□ Other: _____ □ and
weekday parenting time/ visitation on (choose an item):
        □ none
        □ every Wednesday evening.
        □ every other Wednesday evening during the week prior to a non-   visitation weekend
        □ every _____ and _____ evening.
        □ other: _____

_____

For purposes of this Parenting Plan, a weekend will start at _____am/pm on (circle one) Thursday/Friday/Saturday/Other: _____ and end at _____am/pm on (circle one) Sunday/Monday/Other:_____.

Weekday visitation will begin at _____am/pm and will end at (circle one) _____am/pm/ when the child(ren) return(s) to school or day care the next morning/Other:_____

_____

_____.

This parenting schedule begins (check one):

☐ _____ **OR** ☐ **on the date of the Court's Order.**
      (date and time)

B. MAJOR HOLIDAYS AND VACATION PERIODS

THANKSGIVING

The day to day schedule shall apply unless other arrangements are set forth:

_____

beginning _____.

WINTER VACATION

The (choose one) ☐ mother ☐ father shall have the child(ren) for the first period from the day and time school is dismissed until December _____ at _____ am/pm in (choose one) ☐ odd numbered years ☐ even numbered years ☐ every year. The other parent will have the child(ren) for the second period from the day and time indicated above until 6:00 pm on the evening before school resumes. Unless otherwise indicated, the parties shall alternate the first and seconds periods each year.

Other agreement of the parents:

_____

_____

SUMMER VACATION:

Define summer vacation period. Include an explanation of the way that summer camp will be addressed, if applicable. For example, will visitation take priority over camp? If visitation is one week on and one week off, will camp be one week on and one week off?

_____

_____

The day to day schedule shall apply unless other arrangements are set forth:

_____beginning

_____

SPRING VACATION (if applicable):

Define: _____

_____

The day to day schedule shall apply unless other arrangements are set forth:

_____beginning

_____

_____.

FALL VACATION (if applicable):

Define: _____
_____

The day to day schedule shall apply unless other arrangements are set forth:
_____
_____

beginning _____.

C. OTHER HOLIDAY SCHEDULE (if applicable):

Indicate if the child(ren) will be with the parent in ODD or EVEN numbered years or EVERY year:

	MOTHER	FATHER	
Martin Luther King Day			
President's Day			
Mother's Day			
Memorial Day			
Father's Day			
July Fourth			
Labor Day			
Halloween			
Child(ren)'s Birthday			
Mother's Birthday			
Father's Birthday			
Religious Holiday:			
Religious Holiday:			
Religious Holiday:			
Religious Holiday:			
Other:			
Other:			
Other:			

D. OTHER EXTENDED PERIODS OF TIME DURING SCHOOL, ETC. (REFER TO THE SCHOOL SCHEDULE)

_____

_____

E. START AND END DATES FOR HOLIDAY VISITATION:

For the purposes of this Parenting Plan, the holiday will start and end as follows (choose one):
☐ Holidays that fall on Friday will include the following Saturday and Sunday
☐ Holidays that fall on Monday will include the preceding Saturday and Sunday
☐Other: _____
_____

F. <u>COORDINATION OF PARENTING SCHEDULES</u>

Check if applicable:

☐ The holiday parenting time/visitation schedule takes precedence over the regular parenting time/visitation schedule.

☐ When the child(ren) is/are with a parent for an extended parenting time/visitation period (such as summer), the other parent shall be entitled to visit with the child(ren) during the extended period, as follows:

_____

_____

G. <u>TRANSPORTATION ARRANGEMENTS</u>

For visitation, the place of the meeting for the exchange of the child(ren) shall be:

_____

_____

The _____ will be responsible for transportation of the child at the beginning of the visitation.

The _____ will be responsible for transportation of the child at the conclusion of the visitation.

Transportation costs, if any, will be allocated as follows:

_____

_____

Other
provisions:_____

_____

_____

H. <u>CONTACTING THE CHILD</u>

When the child(ren) is/are in the physical custody of one parent, the other parent will have the right to contact the child(ren) as follows:
☐ Telephone
☐ Other: _____

_____
☐ Limitations on contact: _____

_____

I. <u>SUPERVISION OF PARENTING TIME</u> (if applicable):

☐ Check here if applicable
Supervised parenting time shall apply during the day to day schedule as follows:

Place: _____
Person/Organization supervising: _____
Responsibility for cost (check one)   ☐ mother   ☐ father   ☐ both equally

J. COMMUNICATION PROVISIONS

Please check the applicable provision:

□ Each parent shall promptly notify the other parent of a change in address, phone number or cell phone number. A parent changing residence must give at least 30 days notice of the change and provide the full address of the new residence.

□ Due to prior acts of family violence, the address of the child(ren) and victim of family violence shall be kept confidential. The protected parent shall promptly notify the other parent, through a third party, of any change in contact information necessary to conduct visitation.

III. ACCESS TO RECORDS AND INFORMATION

RIGHTS OF THE PARENTS
Absent agreement to limitations of court ordered limitations, pursuant to OCGA § 19-9-1(b)(1)(D), both parents are entitled to access to all of the child(ren)s records and information, including, but not limited to, education, health, extracurricular activities, and religious communications. Designation as a non- custodial parent does not affect a parent's right to equal access to these records.

Limitation on access rights: _____

_____

Other information sharing provisions: _____

_____

IV. MODIFICATION OF PLAN OR DISAGREEMENTS

Parties may, by mutual agreement, vary the parenting time/visitation; however, such agreement shall not be a binding Court Order. Custody shall only be modified by Court Order.

Should the parents disagree about this Parenting Plan or wish to modify it, they must make a good faith effort to resolve the issue between themselves.

V. SPECIAL CONSIDERATIONS

Please attach an addendum detailing any special circumstances of which the Court should be aware (e.g., health issues, educational issues, etc.)

_____

_____

VI. PARENT'S CONSENT

Please review the following and initial:

1. We recognize that a close and continuing parent-child relationship and continuity in the child(ren)'s life is in the child(ren)'s best interest.

Mother's Initial's_____   Father's Initial's _____

2. We recognize that our child(ren)'s needs will change and grow as the child(ren) mature(s); we have made a good faith effort to take these changing needs into account so that the need for future modifications to the Parenting Plan is minimized.

Mother's Initial's_____   Father's Initial's _____

3. We recognize that the parent with physical custody will make the day to day   decisions and emergency decisions while the child is residing with such parent.

Mother's Initial's_____   Father's Initial's _____

☐ We knowingly and voluntarily agree on the terms of this Parenting Plan. Each of us affirms that the information we have provided in this Plan in true and correct.

_____   _____
Father's Signature   **Mother's Signature**

ORDER

The Court has reviewed the foregoing Parenting Plan, and it is hereby made the Order of the Court. This Order entered on _____, _____
_____JUDGE

Guiding Your Clients on Healthy Co-Parenting Skills

Edited by Marti Kitchens-Cobb, LPC, LMFT

Children are affected by the divorce and can actually grow from the experience with parental guidance. Changes such as divorce are an excellent teaching opportunity for children to learn resiliency through change and how to effectively handle conflict. When conflict between parents continues children can fail to adjust properly which can hinder normal emotional development and carry over into their adult lives.

What puts kids at risk for problems?

- The loss or lapse of parenting when children are left to care for themselves
- Disruption to their developmental tasks of "growing up"
- Inability to properly grieve or process the trauma or loss from divorce
- Experience of rejection by a parent can be devastating to a child's self esteem

Divorce is rarely accomplished without some hurt, anger and harsh words. Here are some guidelines for keeping children out of the line of fire between co-parents:

- keep all discussions between co-parents private, do not let children overhear discussions
- keep emotions and opinions of the other parent private and do not discuss them with the child
- if exchanges are difficult without conflict, do them in a neutral, public place
- avoid conflicting messages from different parents, co-parents should communicate often via text messages or voicemail and share all school, vacation, activity and holiday schedules ahead of time to avoid daily interaction or confusion
- do not use the child to pass messages between parents

Helping Children with Two Homes

Co-parents should help each other and the child make and keep established schedules. A helpful activity scheduling/communication tool for co-parents is available online at www.ourfamilywizard.com. Rules for behavior, discipline and consequences should be as similar as possible in both households. Provide the child a specific "space to belong" in each residence such as their own bedroom. Co-parents should also allow the child open communication with the other parent when they are not with them.

Tips for smooth transition exchanges:

- Give the child a 15 minute reminder before they are to be picked up
- Keep exchanges quick and pleasant
- Exchanges are easiest when the child can be retrieved from school, daycare or activities
- Clothing and belongings are often left at the other home so don't make an issue of it
- Always be on time to reduce anxiety for the child and reinforce that they are important to the parent who picks up
- In an emergency or changes due to unforeseen circumstances always communicate with the other co-parent immediately
- Communicate your plans with the co-parent in advance if it requires special clothing/toys

Co-Parent Communication is Key to Success

Communication between co-parents should include courtesy, respect, acceptance and focus on the child's needs and best interests. Even though the family format has changed, as long as the parents share children they will always be a family, just structured differently. As the children mature, co-parents will still want to participate in significant events in the children's lives such as graduations, birthdays, weddings, birth of grandchildren, etc. and establishing a good track record of communication eases the burden for the children.

Co-parents should establish a healthy pattern of problem solving. If they can try to look at their co-parenting relationship as "business partners" it can help minimize the emotional reactions when issues arise. Here is an example of a system to reach resolution:

1) *Establish an agenda*: in advance, arrange to meet to talk with each other regarding the specific item "I'd like to meet with you in the next few days to discuss the summer vacation schedule"
2) *State the issue in very specific terms*: "I'd like to explore the possibility of taking the kids to…."
3) *Ask for what you need* "I will need to ask for time off from work in advance so I need to finalize this as soon as possible"
4) *Do not expect complete cooperation all of the time:* have a back up or alternative plan to offer in case there is resistance
5) *Establish a cooperative pattern*: be proactive in suggesting how parent A can support and help parent B without having to be asked, this sets the tone for a cooperative response when one parent finds themselves in a tight spot
6) *Expect to constantly evaluate and re-negotiate:* having realistic expectations that things change as children grow and their needs and expenses may need adjusting requires flexibility (braces, class trips, college tuition, etc.). Parenting plans should be reviewed regularly to make sure the needs of the children are being met.

When a Co-Parent Won't Cooperate

Refuse to react emotionally to the difficult behavior, set higher standards of cooperation and refuse to engage in the conflict

Plan on difficult behavior and decide in advance how you will handle the situation in a positive way

Be sensitive to what your co-parent is going through and try to put yourself in their position

Examine your own behavior. Is the tone or the words used putting them on the defensive? Are you making blaming, threatening or inflammatory remarks? Work on improving your choice of words

Exercise the golden rule: speak to others as you would have them speak to you

Show your good will: make sure they are invited to events that are important to your child, share pictures, artwork or videos of the child's event that they could not attend

As Parents and Role Models:

- Take responsibility-let kids be kids
- Maintain healthy boundaries with the other parent
- Take good care of yourself, understand and manage your anger
- Develop a business-like attitude when dealing with the other parent
- Seek solutions instead of arguments
- Model good self care, remember you are a role model and mentor for your child
- Respect and value the other parent's role
- Allow your child to openly talk about their parents in each home
- Have your children at the top of your priority list
- Never threaten the other parent in the presence of the children
- Offer love, encouragement and support
- Remain in the parental role and set clear expectations and consistent boundaries

- Give your child permission to know and love the other parent and tell him/her frequently that you love them.
- Allow input in regards to schedules as the child reaches teen years
- Allow your children to grieve the losses associated with change and give them permission to talk about how they feel

Implications for Therapists

Have your client consider counseling for the children at the first sign of regression or behavioral changes. Respect the child's privacy and confidentiality in therapy. Involve both parents in therapy, if possible and educate them about children's needs and the importance of co-parenting. Spend time educating parents about the effects of the conflict on their children. Guide parents in seeing the value in attending to the needs of their children. They must continue to set limits, enforce bedtimes, and assign chores. It has been found that counseling both parents and children before the divorce is believed to help in the transition at the time of separation.

Co-Parents Moving on to New Relationships

Statistics show that 80% of men and 70% of women remarry within 5 years post divorce. Here are tips for parents on how to make sure children can adjust comfortably when parents introduce new relationships into the family.

- When beginning the dating process take it slow, consider your own needs to heal and your children's needs to heal

- The best and most appropriate time to begin dating is when the child is spending time with the other parent. Honor your parenting time with the child to be alone with the child.

- Approach any new relationship with a "friends only" position. Be cautious about jumping into a serious relationship too soon, save alone time for yourself and plenty of time to be alone with the children

- Be aware of your own vulnerability and loneliness that could cloud your vision and result in making a poor choice regarding a new partner

- Your children are fearful of "losing" you to a new "love". Be sure that you are serious about someone before introducing them to your children

- Because children can be easily confused about adult relationships it is not wise to move in with a non- family member of the opposite sex, even if platonic

- When you tell your children about your new relationship, do it when you are alone with your children without the new partner present so that they can talk freely about how they feel

- Proceed slowly when including your new partner in family events because your children need the special time they share with you alone on these occasions

- Keep private time alone with your new partner private. Children feel left out when their parent is holding hands, snuggling or kissing someone else. Until you actually remarry, this is best left out of family time

- Treat your co-parent with dignity and respect and avoid making comments on their new partner or lifestyle

- Make certain that your new partner does not step into a "parenting" role nor attempt to replace the other parent. They will begin their own friendship relationship with them. Your new partner should never be involved in disciplining your children or routinely left to babysit them while you are otherwise engaged

- Be careful not to let your new partner set the rules for you and your children. If you plan to remarry, invest in some pre-marital counseling with a therapist who is skilled in blended families. It is important to move slowly, confidently and unified into a new family structure.

Contributors and Workshop Presenters

Jeri Apple (Amann), LCSW, LMFT, BCC is a (CCE) Board Certified Coach and Adjunct Faculty member for the Federal Executive Institute and works with successful executives and organizations. Jeri helps professionals transform their limiting beliefs and communication anxiety into a powerful presence of charisma while presenting, conducting a meeting, and speaking up when it matters. Jeri's expertise in neuroscience combined with her 30+ years as a coach, a licensed mental health professional and a certified hypnotherapist offers strategies and skills that help successful executives manage fear and anxiety so that they can speak with confidence. In her coaching practice, she is an expert in helping CEO's with stress management and creating a shift in consciousness with purposeful guidance in whole person wellbeing in their personal and professional lives. Jeri is the co-author of the court mandated divorcing parent's seminar, *Children of Divorce©*. This program was one of the first in the state of Georgia and is still utilized by many counties in Georgia, Tennessee and Florida as well as internationally.

Leslie Dinkins, LCSW, earned her Bachelor's in Psychology and her Master's in Social Work both from Georgia State University and currently works for the Forsyth County Accountability Courts Program. She was formerly a domestic violence victim counselor for the Forsyth County Solicitor's Office. She has 14 years experience in the domestic violence field facilitating trainings for a number of professional disciplines and counseling offenders, as well as victims. Her background includes work with domestic violence offenders as a certified FVIP facilitator, conducting individual therapy, and facilitating addiction groups. Leslie is passionate about preventing intimate partner abuse and advocates for the eradication of partner abuse in our society.

Dawn Echols, M.S., L.P.C., earned her master's in Clinical Counseling and Psychology from Brenau University. Prior to becoming a counselor/mediator, Dawn spent 25 years in sales, marketing, and finance, both in corporate and entrepreneurial, as well as managerial, positions. She is the owner & executive director of **Dawning Phoenix, LLC** – a counseling and conflict resolution practice based out of Gainesville, GA. She counsels individuals and couples/partners, as well as groups, for a variety of disorders, with specialties in couples' theory, divorce, anxiety, anger/aggression, and high conflict relationships. Her mediation specialty is divorce. She practices therapy from an Adlerian perspective and often works as a part-time professor of psychology at UNG/Gainesville State College. She has been a certified FVIP facilitator with a specialty in domestic violence, where she conducted original research. Dawn serves in advocacy work for victims of domestic violence and abuse, and is also a GA Registered Neutral Mediator. She has served in volunteer positions for the Forsyth County Domestic Violence Task Force, Family TIES Gainesville, and the Licensed Professional Counselors Association (LPCA) of Georgia. She supports the work of local domestic violence shelters and other organizations that help families prevent, heal, and recover from all forms of difficulties.

Denise Houston, LPC, earned her undergraduate degree from Kennesaw State University in Social/Public Service and Psychology. She earned her Master's Degree in Counseling from Georgia School of Professional Psychology (now Argosy University) in 1996 and is currently in private practice in Cumming, Ga. She enjoys working with people across the life span and sees clients from age 3 to people well into their 80's. Her areas of specialty are recovery from trauma and loss, grief, child abuse and neglect, children of Divorce, adjustment disorders, adoption issues and secondary trauma. She has worked in Child Advocacy Centers providing forensic services in addition to treatment for victims of child abuse and their families, county mental health services, inpatient eating disorders, and enjoys doing trainings for both lay people and professionals who work with trauma-exposed children and adults.

Marti Kitchens-Cobb, M.A., LMFT, LPC, GA Registered Mediator, has been both a mediator and licensed Marriage and Family Therapist for the past 33 years. As a mediator, she is particularly skilled in areas of custody and shared parenting disputes and cases involving parties with difficult personalities. Marti has served on the Boards of Directors of the Family Mediation Association of Georgia, Cobb Mediators Association and is a current member as well as a past president of Georgia Mediators

Association. She also has been appointed, by the Supreme Court, to the Commission of the Georgia Office of Dispute Resolution, just finishing a six year term where she served on the Ethics, Budget and Personnel and Liaison Committees. She is a clinical member of the American Association of Marriage and Family Therapists. Marti is the co-author of the court mandated divorcing parent's seminar, *Children of Divorce©*. This program was one of the first in the state of Georgia and is still utilized by many counties in Georgia, Tennessee and Florida as well as internationally. Over the years, she has presented seminars and workshops both locally and for national organizations. Teaching organizations how to work with difficult people is of particular interest to her. Her company is **Above And Beyond Conflict.** They provide conflict resolution consultation to organizations, workshops for mediators, attorneys, school systems and corporations as well as training and conflict resolution services for agencies and companies. **Above and Beyond Conflict** won a Groundbreaker Award from Atlanta Magazine in 2013 for using Neuroscience in Mediation.

Kelley Linn, Publisher, Educator, Managing Partner **Family Divorce Mediation Centers,** earned her Bachelor of Science in Journalism from Radford University. She has written and published internal procedural manuals for Fortune 500 companies and Non-Profit Charities. After experiencing a very costly and wounding 25 month divorce process, she recognized the need for an instructional manual on how to avoid the pitfalls many families experience through divorce. She created **Transitions Resource, LLC**, a Divorce Consumer Advocacy committed to reducing the wounding of divorce. She compiled and published *Transitions-A Divorce Prep Workbook* (Amazon.com) that guides the family on how to prepare prior to engaging in the legal divorce process. From 2010 through 2014 her organization offered an accredited 19 Core Continuing Education Series called *Advanced Family Divorce Therapy* to the Therapy industry. This educational content is now available in their latest publication *Family Divorce Therapy 101-A Clinicians Guide to Best Practices in Treating Families pre/during/post Divorce* to bring knowledge from seasoned divorce specialists to practitioners to share clinical techniques on how to treat divorcing clients. She has also published *Transitions Resource Recover/Discover Workbook* and *Transitions Resource Recover/Discover in God's Word Workbook*,

(Amazon.com) which are structured 14 session therapy guidebooks used in private session or group therapy. These incorporate concepts of processing introduced in Dr. Jessica Blalock, Ph.D.'s *Discover Yourself-A Personal Development Workbook*. Her current role includes managing multiple Family Divorce Mediation Centers in Atlanta to help reform the method of divorce to a more family-friendly process to minimize the conflict and cost and enhance post divorce co-parenting relations.

Kathleen Shack, LMFT, is an experienced Licensed Marriage and Family Therapist, Collaborative Divorce Coach, Child Specialist, Mediation Coach and Georgia Registered Mediator. She is the owner of Family Solutions Counseling, LLC and has been in private practice since 2000. In therapy sessions she helps children and adults gain understanding and navigate through the dynamics of their family. During Discernment Counseling, she helps couples gain clarity and confidence about next steps in their relationship while also gaining a deeper understanding of what has happened in the marriage. With divorcing families she works with parents as they develop healthy co-parenting skills and provides insight to parents regarding their child's needs before, during and after divorce. Kathleen uses therapeutic skills and knowledge to support, educate and prepare clients for the successful negotiation of a divorce settlement agreement. Coaching helps to reduce the emotional intensity of the divorce and helps the client separate legal and practical issues from emotional issues. As a Registered Domestic/Divorce Mediator, she facilitates confidential resolution between divorcing individuals and helps parents develop a Parenting Plan regarding their children.

Helpful Books and Articles

Divorce

Transitions Divorce Prep Workbook-Transitions Resource
The High Road Has Less Traffic-Monique A. Honaman
Splitting – Protecting Yourself While Divorcing a Narcissist – Bill Eddy
Hanging on by My Fingernails, *How a Scratch Can Land You in Jail* – Janie McQueen
Transitions Resource Recover/Discover-Transitions Resource
What do Divorce Lawyers do In their Own Divorces-Huffpost 2/9/2012- Kulerski & Cornelison

Relational Afflictions

From Charm to Harm-Amy Lewis Bear
Verbal Abuse Survivors Speak Out – Patricia Evans
When Dad Hurts Mom – Lundy Bancroft
The Betrayal Bond, Breaking Free of Exploitive Relationships – Carnes
Deceived, Facing Sexual Betrayal, Lies and Secrets – Claudia Black
Mending a Shattered Heart – Carnes

Spiritual Based Inspirational Books for Clients

Transitions Resource Recover/Discover in God's Word-Transitions Resource
God Calling – A.J. Russell
Why? – Anne Graham Lotz
Fool-Proofing Your Life – Jan Silvious

Made in the USA
Charleston, SC
30 July 2015